# *The Illustrated*
# Longitude

# The Illustrated
# Longitude

## DAVA SOBEL
### AND
## WILLIAM J. H. ANDREWES

Fourth Estate • *London*

*For my mother,*
*Betty Gruber Sobel,*
*a four-star navigator*
*who can sail by the heavens*
*but always drives by way of Canarsie*

— D. S.


*For my parents,*
*John and Pol Andrewes,*
*my haven throughout the voyage*

— W. A.

This paperback edition first published in 1999
First published in Great Britain in 1998 by
Fourth Estate Limited
6 Salem Road
London W2 4BU

10 9 8 7 6 5 4 3 2 1

A catalogue record for this book is available from the British Library.

ISBN 1-84115-233-1

Design by Robert Updegraff
Colour separations by Rapida Group, plc, London
Printed in Italy by LEGO, Vicenza

# Contents

# Acknowledgments

The authors offer their special thanks to Catherine Andrewes, Jonathan Betts, Michael Carlisle, Bruce Chandler, George Gibson, Owen Gingerich, Derek Howse, Andrew King, David Landes, Peggy Liversidge, David Penney, and Martha Richardson for their useful comments to the text and captions.

The following individuals have contributed in many other important ways:

Diane Ackerman; Pippa Andrewes; Art Resource, New York: Alison Gallup; Ashmolean Museum, Oxford: Anne Steinberg; Ellen Bruce Atkins; David Axelrod; Rear-Admiral François Bellec; Mario Biagioli; Biblioteca Nazionale Centrale, Florence: Carla Giuducci Bonanni; Bibliothèque Nationale de France, Paris: Marie-Thérèse Gousset; Bodleian Library, Oxford; The Boston Athenaeum: Catherine Cooper, Richard Wendorf; Bridgeman Art Library, London & New York: Lesley Black, Adrian Gibbs, Alice Whitehead; British Library, London: Nicola Beech, Gwen Gittings; The British Museum, London: David Thompson; Martin Burgess; Cambridge University Library, Royal Greenwich Observatory Archives: D.J. Hall, Ruth Long, Adam J. Perkins; Catherine Cardinal; Christ's Hospital, Horsham: Dot Mariner, N.M. Plumley; Collection of Historical Scientific Instruments, Harvard University; Conservatoire National des Arts et Métiers, Paris: Frédérique Desvergnes, Nathalie Naudi; George Daniels; Fiftieth Space Wing Public Affairs, Falcon Air Force Base, Colorado: Bill Bollwerk, Mary Hinson, Steve Hutsell; Fourth Estate: Victoria Barnsley, Graham Cook, Paul Forty, Victoria Heyworth-Dunne, Christopher Potter; Charles Frodsham & Co., London: Richard Stenning, Philip Whyte; Göttingen University Library (Staatsarchiv Hannover); John Griffiths; Harvard Law School Library: David Warrington; *Harvard Magazine*: John Bethell, Janet Hawkins, Jean Martin, Christopher Reed; Harvard Map Collection: David Cobb, Joseph Garver, Arlene Olivero; Harvard University Art Museums: Marie Clare Altenhofen, Marjorie Cohn, Elizabeth Gombosi, Elizabeth Mitchell; Anders Hedberg; Houghton Library, Harvard University: Anne Anninger, Tom Ford, Roger Stoddard; Huygensmuseum Hofwijck, The Netherlands: Maria Arts Vehmeyer; Istituto e Museo di Storia della Scienza, Florence: Mara Miniati, Franca Principe; Isaac Klein; Zoë Klein; Ladygate Antiques, Beverly, U.K.: Lew and Pat Goodman; Heather Lees; John H. Leopold; Michael S. Mahoney; Tony Mercer; Musée de la Marine, Paris: Delphine Allannic; Museum Boerhaave, Leiden: Peter de Clercq, Robert van Gent; National Association of Watch and Clock Collectors, Columbia, Pa.: Beth Bisbano, Eileen Doudna, Kathy Everett; National Maritime Museum: Maria Blyzinski, Gloria Clifton, Kristen Lippincott, Lindsey Macfarlane, Richard Ormond, Colin Starkey, David Taylor; National Portrait Gallery: Bernard Horrocks, Jill Springall; Nederlands Scheepvaartmuseum: Diederik Wildeman, Willem Mörzer Bruyns; Observatoire de Paris: J. Alexandre, Suzanne Débarbat; Öffentliche Kunstsammlung Basel, Kunstmuseum: Charlotte Gutzwiller; Ole Roemer Museum, Denmark: Claus Thykier; Mariana Oller; Patent Office, London; The Pepys Library, Magdalene College, Cambridge: Aude Fitzsimons; Steve Pitkin; Fred Powell; Anthony G. Randall; Royal Collection Enterprises: Sarah Blake, Shruti Patel, Nicole Tetzner; P. J. Rogers; Royal Society: Sandra Cumming, Samantha Eley; Amanda Sobel; Stephen Sobel; Science Museum, London: Kevin Johnson, Alan Morton; Science Museum/Science and Society Picture Library, London: Venita Paul; Alan Neale Stimson; Jan Tadrup; Norman J. W. Thrower; The Time Museum, Rockford, Illinois: Patricia Atwood, Seth Atwood, Ann Shallcross, John Shallcross; Trinity College, Cambridge: Alison Sprospon; A. J. Turner; United Technologies Corporation: Marie Dalton-Meyer, Lawrence Gavrich; University Library, Leiden, Department of Western Manuscripts: R. Breugelmans; Robert Updegraff; Usher Gallery, Lincoln: Judith Robinson, Richard Wood; U.S. Naval Observatory, Washington, D.C.: Geoff Chester, Stephen Dick; Burton Van Deusen; Albert Van Helden; Robert Vessot; Walker and Company: Vicki Haire, Ivy Hamlin, Marlene Tungseth; Jeffrey L. Ward Graphic Design: Jeffrey Ward; Widener Library Imaging Services, Harvard University: Stephen Sylvester, Robert Zinck; William Andrews Clark Memorial Library, UCLA: John Bidwell; Worshipful Company of Clockmakers: Christopher Clarke, Sir George White; Yale Center for British Art: Marilyn Hunt, Maria Rossi; The Earl of Yarborough

# Introduction

In the exciting years since the publication of *Longitude*, many thoughtful readers have commented—while others complained—about the lack of pictures or diagrams to vivify the story. Therefore I am delighted now to introduce this handsome new illustrated volume and to welcome my good friend William J. H. Andrewes as its coauthor.

Will and I met each other over an exhibit of astrolabes at Chicago's Adler Planetarium in February 1992, but the subject soon turned to longitude. Will, as curator of Harvard University's Collection of Historical Scientific Instruments, invited me, a science writer, to report on the Longitude Symposium he planned to host nearly two years later in Cambridge, Massachusetts. I hoped to attend the three-day event and write an article about it for a popular magazine. Editors I approached at numerous periodicals, however, expressed the unanimous sentiment that the concept was esoteric in the extreme, and none could imagine who would want to read about it. After months of unsuccessful petitioning, I finally found a home for my idea at *Harvard Magazine* just a few days before the symposium started.

I arrived on campus to discover some five hundred participants, many of them members of the National Association of Watch and Clock Collectors, observing the tercentenary of a relatively uncelebrated English genius named John Harrison, who, by the mid-1700s, had almost single-handedly solved the age-old longitude problem by perfecting the art of portable precision timekeeping. Will, long a champion of Harrison's, had looked after the clocks at the Old Royal Observatory and the National Maritime Museum in Greenwich, England, where Harrison's treasures are exhibited, and had restored to working order an early wooden clock that Harrison never finished. In addition to the three-century travelogue of slides shown during the symposium lectures, along with colorful animated videos of Harrison's mechanisms, Will's conference included a viewing of important clocks from the Harvard collection. He thoughtfully extracted the interiors from most of these instruments so that their ornate wood and metal cases stood empty beside their revealed works.

From our experiences at the Longitude Symposium, Will and I each created a book. His, *The Quest for Longitude*, featured the full formal proceedings of all the sessions, annotated and illustrated in wonderful detail. Mine, shorter and smaller in scope, focused on Harrison's struggle with the intractable problem and the even more intractable authorities dead set against him. In the following pages of our joint venture, the original *Longitude* text unfolds among 180 images of characters, events, instruments (especially Harrison's contrivances), maps, and publications that illuminate the narrative. These pictures, paired with Will's detailed captions, offer up their own version of a swashbuckling scientific adventure in the context of history and technology.

— DAVA SOBEL

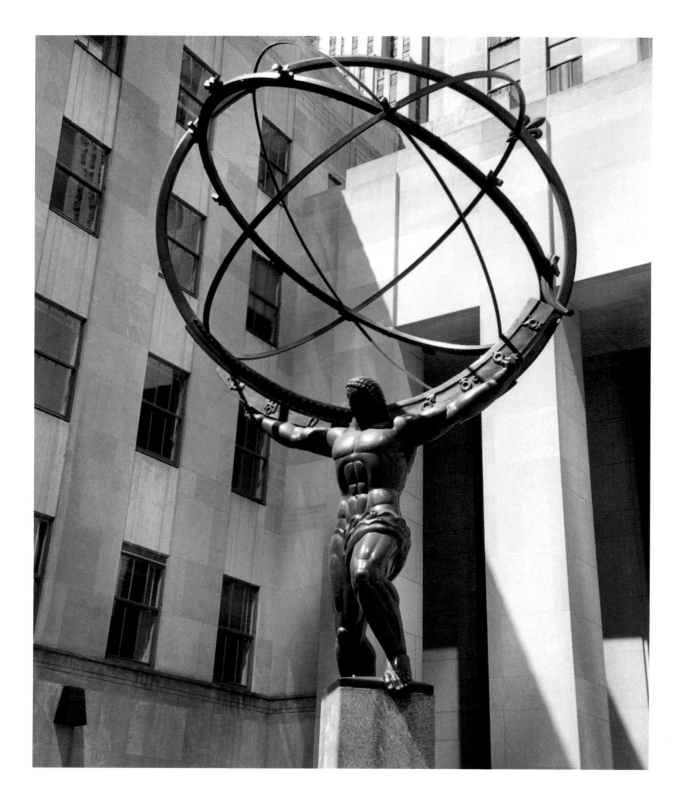

## CHAPTER ONE

# *Imaginary Lines*

When I'm playful I use the meridians of
longitude and parallels of latitude for a seine,
and drag the Atlantic Ocean for whales.

MARK TWAIN, *Life on the Mississippi*

ONCE ON A WEDNESDAY excursion when I was a little girl, my father bought me a beaded wire ball that I loved. At a touch, I could collapse the toy into a flat coil between my palms, or pop it open to make a hollow sphere. Rounded out, it resembled a tiny Earth, because its hinged wires traced the same pattern of intersecting circles that I had seen on the globe in my schoolroom — the thin black lines of latitude and longitude. The few colored beads slid along the wire paths haphazardly, like ships on the high seas.

My father strode up Fifth Avenue to Rockefeller Center with me on his shoulders, and we stopped to stare at the statue of Atlas, carrying Heaven and Earth on his.

The bronze orb that Atlas held aloft, like the wire toy in my hands, was a see-through world, defined by imaginary lines. The Equator. The Ecliptic. The Tropic of Cancer. The Tropic of Capricorn. The Arctic Circle. The prime meridian. Even then I could recognize, in the graph-paper grid imposed on the globe, a powerful symbol of all the real lands and waters on the planet.

*Lee Lawrie's forty-five-foot high statue of Atlas was erected in 1937 at the Rockefeller Center's International Building on Fifth Avenue, New York City.*

*Lines of latitude and longitude were introduced as a means of defining the location of any place on the Earth's surface. Latitudes are marked by the parallel lines encircling the Earth, from zero degrees on the equator to ninety degrees at the poles. Longitudes, running from pole to pole, divide the 360-degree circle of the Equator. Cartographers placed the prime, or zero, meridian at the point from which longitude was to be measured. In this illustration from a 1549 French manuscript edition of Oronce Fine's* Sphaera Mundi, *the lines of latitude and longitude are spaced at intervals of five degrees.*

Today, the latitude and longitude lines govern with more authority than I could have imagined forty-odd years ago, for they stay fixed as the world changes its configuration underneath them—with continents adrift across a widening sea, and national boundaries repeatedly redrawn by war or peace.

As a child, I learned the trick for remembering the difference between latitude and longitude. The latitude lines, the parallels, really do stay

parallel to each other as they girdle the globe from the Equator to the poles in a series of shrinking concentric rings. The meridians of longitude go the other way: They loop from the North Pole to the South and back again in great circles of the same size, so they all converge at the ends of the Earth.

Lines of latitude and longitude began crisscrossing our worldview in ancient times, at least three centuries before the birth of Christ. By A.D. 150, the cartographer and astronomer Ptolemy had plotted them on the twenty-seven maps of his first world atlas. Also for this landmark volume, Ptolemy listed all the place names in an index, in alphabetical order, with the latitude and longitude of each—as well as he could gauge them from travelers' reports. Ptolemy himself had only an armchair appreciation of the wider world. A common misconception of his day held that anyone living below the Equator would melt into deformity from the horrible heat.

The Equator marked the zero-degree parallel of latitude for Ptolemy. He did not choose it arbitrarily but took it on higher authority from his predecessors, who had derived it from nature while observing the motions of the heavenly bodies. The sun, moon, and planets pass almost directly overhead at the Equator. Likewise the Tropic of Cancer and the Tropic of Capricorn, two other famous parallels, assume their positions at the sun's command. They mark the northern and southern boundaries of the sun's apparent motion over the course of the year.

Ptolemy was free, however, to lay his prime meridian, the zero-degree longitude line, wherever he liked. He chose to run it through the Fortunate Islands (now called the Canary Islands) off the northwest coast of Africa. Later mapmakers moved the prime meridian to the Azores and to the Cape Verde Islands, as well as to Rome,

*World map from the 1482 edition of Claudius Ptolemy's* Cosmographia. *Ptolemy's prime meridian ran through the westernmost point of known civilization, the Fortunate Islands or Isles of the Blest, which correspond today with the Canary Islands.*

*This world map from the 1513 edition of Ptolemy's* Geographia *illustrates the remarkable progress in cartography that had occurred in the three decades since the publication of the 1482 edition. The original title of this book,* Cosmographia, *was changed in 1507 to* Geographia. *This was more descriptive of its contents, which were constantly being revised to incorporate new discoveries and improvements in geographical knowledge.*

*In this map of the Western (Atlantic) Ocean, from the 1513 edition of Ptolemy's* Geographia, *the most recent discoveries of the "New World" are depicted. Although mariners became familiar with the latitudes of various landfalls in the New World as oceanic voyages increased, much of the published information about the location of islands, and even continents, and the delineation of the coastlines remained highly inaccurate, perhaps to protect the knowledge of their true position: The Tropic of Cancer (25½ degrees), shown here to run just south of Spagnolia (Haiti and the Dominican Republic), lies, in fact, just north of Isabella (Cuba). Mariners searching for Isabella in the latitude of twenty-eight degrees to thirty-six degrees north, as shown on this map, would find themselves on the coast of the Carolinas and Florida, anywhere between 400 and 1,000 miles north of its actual location.*

Copenhagen, Jerusalem, St. Petersburg, Pisa, Paris, and Philadelphia, among other places, before it settled down at last in London. As the world turns, any line drawn from pole to pole may serve as well as any other for a starting line of reference. The placement of the prime meridian is a purely political decision.

Here lies the real, hard-core difference between latitude and longitude—beyond the superficial difference in line direction that any child can see: The zero-degree parallel of latitude is fixed by the laws of nature, while the zero-degree meridian of longitude shifts like the sands of time. This difference makes finding latitude child's play, and turns the determination of longitude, especially at sea, into an adult dilemma—one that stumped the wisest minds of the world for the better part of human history.

Any sailor worth his salt can gauge his latitude well enough by the length of the day, or by the height of the sun or known guide stars above the horizon. Christopher Columbus

*The Earth's orbit around the sun and the tilt of its axis create the seasons and the imaginary lines of the Equator and the Tropics. When the sun passes over the equator on March 20 (the spring equinox), it appears from Earth to enter the sign of Aries. On June 21 (the summer solstice), the sun appears to enter the sign of Cancer as it passes over the Tropic of Cancer. In September at the autumnal equinox, the sun crosses the Equator southward and enters the sign of Libra, and the winter solstice in December brings the sun to its farthest point south of the Equator, over the Tropic of Capricorn.*

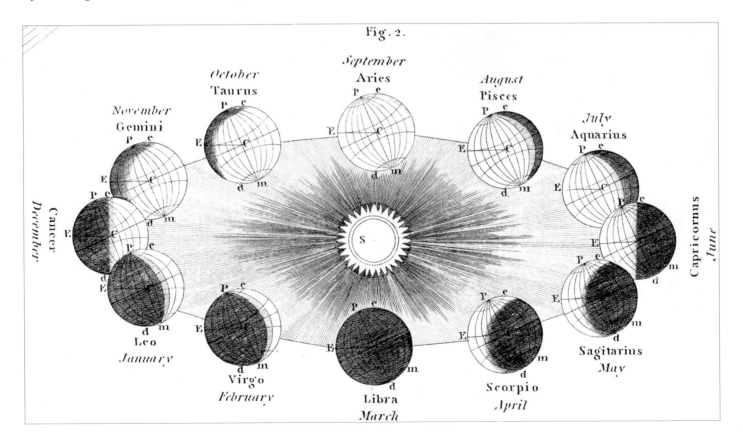

Fig. 2.

# MEASURING LONGITUDE

Published in the first edition of the *Encyclopedia Britannica* in 1771, this table shows how one degree of longitude represents sixty nautical miles on the Equator and steadily reduces its value to zero at the poles as the degrees of latitude (D. L.) increase.

| D.L. | Miles | D.L. | Miles | D.L. | Miles | D.L. | Miles | D.L. | Miles |
|---|---|---|---|---|---|---|---|---|---|
| 1 | 59.99 | 19 | 56.73 | 37 | 47.92 | 55 | 34.41 | 73 | 17.54 |
| 2 | 59.97 | 20 | 50.38 | 38 | 47.28 | 56 | 33.55 | 74 | 16.53 |
| 3 | 59.92 | 21 | 56.01 | 39 | 46.62 | 57 | 32.68 | 75 | 15.52 |
| 4 | 59.86 | 22 | 55.63 | 40 | 45.95 | 58 | 31.74 | 76 | 14.51 |
| 5 | 59.77 | 23 | 55.23 | 41 | 45.28 | 59 | 30.90 | 77 | 13.50 |
| 6 | 59.67 | 24 | 54.81 | 42 | 44.95 | 60 | 30.00 | 78 | 12.48 |
| 7 | 59.56 | 25 | 54.38 | 43 | 43.88 | 61 | 29.09 | 79 | 11.45 |
| 8 | 59.42 | 26 | 53.93 | 44 | 43.16 | 62 | 28.17 | 80 | 10.42 |
| 9 | 59.26 | 27 | 53.46 | 45 | 42.43 | 63 | 27.24 | 81 | 9.38 |
| 10 | 59.08 | 28 | 52.97 | 46 | 51.68 | 64 | 26.30 | 82 | 8.35 |
| 11 | 58.89 | 29 | 52.47 | 47 | 40.92 | 65 | 25.36 | 83 | 7.32 |
| 12 | 58.68 | 30 | 51.96 | 48 | 40.15 | 66 | 24.41 | 84 | 6.28 |
| 13 | 58.46 | 31 | 51.43 | 49 | 39.36 | 67 | 23.45 | 85 | 5.23 |
| 14 | 58.22 | 32 | 50.88 | 50 | 38.57 | 68 | 22.48 | 86 | 4.18 |
| 15 | 57.95 | 33 | 50.32 | 51 | 37.76 | 69 | 21.50 | 87 | 3.14 |
| 16 | 57.67 | 34 | 49.74 | 52 | 36.94 | 70 | 20.52 | 88 | 2.09 |
| 17 | 57.37 | 35 | 49.15 | 53 | 36.11 | 71 | 19.54 | 89 | 1.05 |
| 18 | 57.06 | 36 | 48.54 | 54 | 35.26 | 72 | 18.55 | 90 | 0.00 |

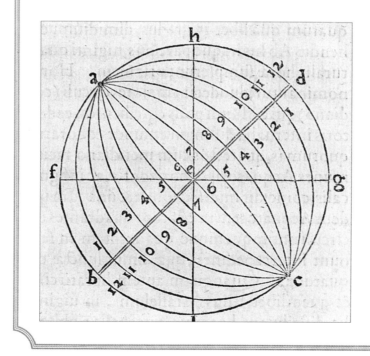

The Earth rotates 360 degrees in twenty-four hours, fifteen degrees per hour, or one degree every four minutes. This mid-sixteenth-century illustration, with the lines of longitude spaced at intervals of fifteen degrees and marked for each hour of the day, demonstrates how a difference in longitude can be expressed by the difference in time.

followed a straight path across the Atlantic when he "sailed the parallel" on his 1492 journey, and the technique would doubtless have carried him to the Indies had not the Americas intervened.

The measurement of longitude meridians, in comparison, is tempered by time. To learn one's longitude at sea, one needs to know what time it is aboard ship and also the time at the home port or another place of known longitude — at that very same moment. The two clock times enable the navigator to convert the hour difference into a geographical separation. Since the Earth takes twenty-four hours to complete one full revolution of three hundred sixty degrees, one hour marks one twenty-fourth of a spin, or fifteen degrees. And so each hour's time difference between the ship and the starting point marks a progress of fifteen degrees of longitude to the east or west. Every day at sea, when the navigator resets his ship's clock to local noon as the sun reaches its highest point in the sky, and then consults the home-port clock, every hour's discrepancy between them translates into another fifteen degrees of longitude.

Those same fifteen degrees of longitude also correspond to a distance traveled. At the Equator, where the girth of the Earth is greatest, fifteen degrees stretch fully one thousand miles. North or south of that line, however, the mileage value of each degree decreases. One degree of longitude equals four minutes of time the world over, but in terms of distance, one degree shrinks from sixty-eight miles at the Equator to virtually nothing at the poles.

Precise knowledge of the hour in two different places at once — a longitude prerequisite so easily accessible today from any pair of cheap wristwatches — was utterly unattainable up to and including the era of pendulum clocks. On the deck of a rolling ship, such clocks would slow down, or speed up, or stop running altogether. Normal changes in temperature encountered en route from a cold country of origin to a tropical trade zone thinned or thickened a clock's lubricating oil and made its metal parts expand or contract with equally disastrous results. A rise or fall in barometric pressure, or the subtle variations in the Earth's gravity from one latitude to another, could also cause a clock to gain or lose time.

*This map shows the basic currents and winds of the North and South Atlantic, which, along with seasonal weather patterns, influence the course of voyages.*

For lack of a practical method of determining longitude, every great captain in the Age of Exploration became lost at sea despite the best available charts and compasses. From Vasco da Gama to Vasco Núñez de Balboa, from Ferdinand Magellan to Sir Francis Drake—they all got where they were going willy-nilly, by forces attributed to good luck or the grace of God.

As more and more sailing vessels set out to conquer or explore new territories, to wage war, or to ferry gold and commodities between foreign lands, the wealth of nations floated upon the oceans. And still no ship owned a reliable means for establishing her whereabouts. In consequence, untold numbers of sailors died when their destinations suddenly loomed out of the sea and took them by surprise. In a single such accident, on October 22, 1707, at the Scilly Isles four homebound British warships ran aground and nearly two thousand men lost their lives.

The active quest for a solution to the problem of longitude persisted over four centuries and across the whole continent of Europe. Most crowned heads of state eventually played a part in the longitude story, notably George III and Louis XIV. Seafaring men such as Captain William Bligh of the *Bounty* and the great circumnavigator Captain James Cook, who made three long voyages of exploration and experimentation before his violent death in Hawaii, took the more promising methods to sea to test their accuracy and practicability.

Renowned astronomers approached the longitude challenge by appealing to the clockwork universe: Galileo Galilei, Jean-Dominique Cassini, Christiaan Huygens, Sir Isaac Newton, and Edmond Halley, of comet fame, all entreated the moon and stars for help. Palatial observatories were founded at Paris, London, and Berlin for the express purpose of determining longitude by the heavens. Meanwhile, lesser minds devised schemes that depended on the yelps of wounded dogs, or the cannon blasts of signal ships strategically anchored—somehow—on the open ocean.

In the course of their struggle to find longitude, scientists struck upon other discoveries that changed their view of the universe. These include the first accurate determinations of the weight of the Earth, the distance to the stars, and the speed of light.

As time passed and no method proved successful, the search for a solution to the longitude problem assumed legendary proportions, on a par with discovering the Fountain of Youth, the secret of perpetual motion, or the formula for transforming lead into gold. The governments of the great maritime nations—including Spain, the Netherlands, and certain city-states of Italy—periodically roiled the fervor by offering jackpot purses for a workable method. The British Parliament, in its famed Longitude Act of 1714, set the highest bounty of all, naming a prize equal to a king's ransom (several million dollars in today's currency) for a "Practicable and Useful" means of determining longitude.

English clockmaker John Harrison, a mechanical genius who pioneered the science of portable precision timekeeping, devoted his life to this quest. He accomplished what Newton had feared was impossible: He invented a clock that would carry the true time from the home port, like an eternal flame, to any remote corner of the world.

Harrison, a man of simple birth and high intelligence, crossed swords with the leading lights of his day. He made a special enemy of the Reverend

*These voyages of five famous explorers show how the courses of their voyages were influenced to some extent by the currents and winds. The trade route that became established between England and the Caribbean islands and the colonies in the southern part of North America followed the Canary and the North Equatorial currents on the journey out and the Gulf Stream on the return.*

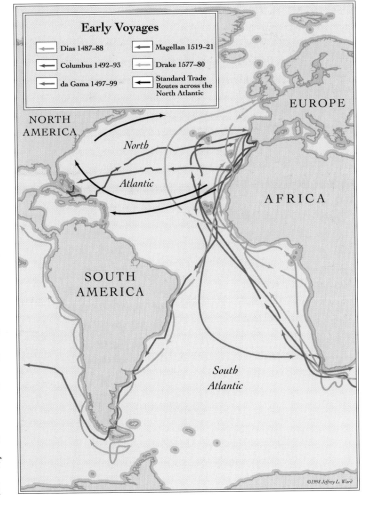

**Early Voyages**

- ← Dias 1487–88
- ← Columbus 1492–93
- ← da Gama 1497–99
- ← Magellan 1519–21
- ← Drake 1577–80
- ← Standard Trade Routes across the North Atlantic

NORTH AMERICA

EUROPE

North

Atlantic

AFRICA

SOUTH AMERICA

South Atlantic

©1998 Jeffrey L. Ward

Before reliable charts and accurate methods of navigation were introduced, sailors had to rely upon dead reckoning, a calculated estimate of the position of the ship in relation to land. The cost of ignorance was high: Sometimes it resulted in a prolonged voyage with an outbreak of scurvy or other diseases that claimed the lives of seamen. All too often the voyage ended in disaster, when the ship was swept upon the rocks of an unexpected landfall, as shown in this painting of the wreck of the *Dutch East Indiaman*, the Amsterdam, *about 1599.*

The title page of the 1586 Latin edition of Lucas Janszoon Waghenaer's Spieghel der Zeevaerdt *depicts various contemporary navigational aids, including the quadrant, the mariner's astrolabe, and the cross-staff, three instruments commonly used for measuring the height of the sun or stars above the horizon to find latitude. Waghenaer, an experienced navigator, wrote this book as a guide to sailing along the coasts of western Europe. After its publication in England in 1588 under the* title The Mariners Mirrour, *nautical charts became commonly known as "wagoners."*

Nevil Maskelyne, the fifth astronomer royal, who contested his claim to the coveted prize money, and whose tactics at certain junctures can only be described as foul play.

With no formal education or apprenticeship to any watchmaker, Harrison nevertheless constructed a series of virtually friction-free clocks that required no lubrication and no cleaning, that were made from materials impervious to rust, and that kept their moving parts perfectly balanced in relation to one another, regardless of how the world pitched or tossed about them. He did away with the pendulum, and he combined different metals inside his works in such a way that when one component expanded or contracted with changes in temperature, the other counteracted the change and kept the clock's rate constant.

His every success, however, was parried by members of the scientific elite, who distrusted Harrison's magic box. The commissioners charged with awarding the longitude prize—Nevil Maskelyne among them—changed the contest rules whenever they saw fit, so as to favor the chances of astronomers over the likes of Harrison and his fellow "mechanics." But the utility and accuracy of Harrison's approach triumphed in the end. His followers shepherded Harrison's intricate, exquisite invention through the design modifications that enabled it to be mass produced and enjoy wide use.

An aged, exhausted Harrison, taken under the wing of King George III, ultimately claimed his rightful monetary reward in 1773—after forty struggling years of political intrigue, international warfare, academic backbiting, scientific revolution, and economic upheaval.

All these threads, and more, entwine in the lines of longitude. To unravel them now—to retrace their story in an age when a network of orbiting satellites can nail down a ship's position within a few feet in just a moment or two—is to see the globe anew.

*The layout of a log book in columnar form, recommended by Captain John Davis in his famous work* The Seamans Secrets. *The remarks column on the right contains mostly observations of the variation of the compass, the difference between true north and magnetic north.*

## CHAPTER TWO

# The Sea Before Time

They that go down to the Sea in Ships,
that do business in great waters, these
see the works of the Lord, and His
wonders in the deep.

PSALM 107

"DIRTY WEATHER," Admiral Sir Clowdisley Shovell called the fog that had dogged him twelve days at sea. Returning home victorious from Gibraltar after skirmishes with the French Mediterranean forces, Sir Clowdisley could not beat the heavy autumn overcast. Fearing the ships might founder on coastal rocks, the admiral summoned all his navigators to put their heads together.

The consensus opinion placed the English fleet safely west of Île d'Ouessant, an island outpost of the Brittany peninsula. But as the sailors continued north, they discovered to their horror that they had misgauged their position near the Scilly Isles. These tiny islands, about twenty miles from the southwest tip of England, point to Land's End like a path of stepping-stones. And on that foggy night of October 22, 1707, the Scillies became unmarked tombstones for almost two thousand of Sir Clowdisley's troops.

The flagship, the *Association*, struck first. She sank within minutes, drowning all hands. Before the rest of the vessels could react to the obvious danger, two more ships, the *Eagle* and the *Romney*, pricked themselves on the rocks and went down like stones. In all, four warships were lost.

*Sir Clowdisley Shovell (c. 1650-1707) had a distinguished career in the Royal Navy. He rose to the rank of rear admiral by the time he was forty-two and was appointed commander in chief of the British fleets at fifty-four, in 1704. This portrait was painted around 1702.*

Only two men washed ashore alive. One of them was Sir Clowdisley himself, who may have watched the fifty-seven years of his life flash before his eyes as the waves carried him home. Certainly he had time to reflect on the events of the previous twenty-four hours, when he made what must have been the worst mistake in judgment of his naval career. He had been approached by a sailor, a member of the *Association's*

*In October 1707, a fleet of twenty-one ships under the command of Sir Clowdisley Shovell returned from the Mediterranean after an unsuccessful attack on Toulon. The journey home was rough. By October 22, when the fleet's position was estimated to be west of Île d'Ouessant ("Ushent" on this map), orders were given to proceed into the English Channel. As night fell, ignorant of the fate that lay ahead, the ships were driven by strong winds onto the Western Rocks, southwest of St. Agnes in the Scilly Isles ("Silly" on this map). The location of the fleet was not the only unknown: This map, printed thirteen years after the accident, shows the latitude of St. Agnes to be fifty degrees; its actual location is about eight miles further south.*

crew, who claimed to have kept his own reckoning of the fleet's location during the whole cloudy passage. Such subversive navigation by an inferior was forbidden in the Royal Navy, as the unnamed seaman well knew. However, the danger appeared so enormous, by his calculations, that he risked his neck to make his concerns known to the officers. Admiral Shovell had the man hanged for mutiny on the spot.

No one was around to spit "I told you so!" into Sir Clowdisley's face as he nearly drowned. But as soon as the admiral collapsed on dry sand, a local woman combing the beach purportedly found his body and fell in love with the emerald ring on his finger. Between her desire and his depletion, she handily murdered him for it. Three decades later, on her deathbed, this same woman confessed the crime to her clergyman, producing the ring as proof of her guilt and contrition.

*At eight o'clock on the night of October 22, Sir Clowdisley Shovell's ship, the Association, struck the rocks of the Gilstone Ledges in the Scilly Isles and sank in four minutes with its entire crew of 650 men. Two other ships suffered the same fate and a fourth sank more slowly. Only twenty-six men were saved; 1,647 perished. This disaster, caused by errors in finding both latitude and longitude, brought the longitude problem to the attention of the British Parliament.*

The demise of Sir Clowdisley's fleet capped a long saga of seafaring in the days before sailors could find their longitude. Page after page from this miserable history relates quintessential horror stories of death by scurvy and thirst, of ghosts in the rigging, and of landfalls in the form of shipwrecks, with hulls dashed on rocks and heaps of drowned corpses fouling the beaches. In literally hundreds of instances, a vessel's ignorance of her longitude led swiftly to her destruction.

Launched on a mix of bravery and greed, the sea captains of the fifteenth, sixteenth, and seventeenth centuries relied on "dead reckoning" to gauge their distance east or west of home port. The captain would throw a log overboard and observe how quickly the ship receded from this temporary guidepost. He noted the crude speedometer reading in his ship's logbook, along with the direction of travel, which he took from the stars or a compass, and the length of time on a particular course, counted with a sandglass or a pocket watch. Factoring in the effects of ocean currents, fickle winds, and

*Distance traveled at sea was measured by a log (a flat, triangular-shaped piece of wood) attached to the end of a knotted line. Beginning at sixty feet from the log, knots were tied at regular intervals of fifty-one feet. When the log was cast over the side of the ship, the number of knots counted in a period of thirty seconds (measured by a sandglass) would indicate the speed of the ship. Hence the term* knot *was adopted as the nautical measure of speed. This task required three people, one to hold the heavy reel, one to turn the sandglass, and one to count the knots.*

The earliest Western references to the compass date from the twelfth century, and these appear to have taken the form of magnetized needles floating directly on water. The dry-pivoted compass is mentioned in 1269 and the compass card in 1380. The latter became commonly employed for navigation, because, unlike the needle, it could not become dislodged from its pivot. This detail from an early-fifteenth-century French manuscript shows a mariner adjusting the index of a dry-pivoted compass.

errors in judgment, he then determined his longitude. He routinely missed his mark, of course—searching in vain for the island where he had hoped to find fresh water, or even the continent that was his destination. Too often, the technique of dead reckoning marked him for a dead man.

Long voyages waxed longer for lack of longitude, and the extra time at sea condemned sailors to the dread disease of scurvy. The oceangoing diet of the day, devoid of fresh fruits and vegetables, deprived them of vitamin C, and their bodies' connective tissue deteriorated as a result. Their blood vessels leaked, making the men look bruised all over, even in the absence of any injury. When they were injured, their wounds failed to heal. Their legs swelled. They suffered the pain of spontaneous hemorrhaging into their muscles and joints. Their gums bled, too, as their teeth loosened. They gasped for breath, struggled against debilitating weakness, and when the blood vessels around their brains ruptured, they died.

Beyond this potential for human suffering, the global ignorance of longitude wreaked economic havoc on the grandest scale. It confined oceangoing vessels to a few narrow shipping lanes that promised safe passage. Forced to navigate by latitude alone, whaling ships, merchant ships, warships, and pirate ships all clustered along well-trafficked routes, where they fell prey to one another. In 1592, for example, a squadron of six English men-of-war coasted off the Azores, lying in ambush for Spanish traders heading back from the Caribbean. The *Madre de Deus*, an enormous Portuguese galleon returning from India, sailed into their web. Despite her thirty-two brass guns, the *Madre de Deus* lost the brief battle, and Portugal lost a princely cargo. Under the ship's hatches lay chests of gold and silver coins, pearls, diamonds, amber, musk, tapestries, calico, and ebony. The spices had to be counted by the ton—more than four hundred tons of pepper, forty-five of cloves, thirty-five of cinnamon, and three each of mace and nutmeg. The *Madre de Deus* proved herself a prize worth half a million pounds sterling—or approximately half the net value of the entire English Exchequer at that date.

By the end of the seventeenth century, nearly three hundred ships a year sailed between the British Isles and the West Indies to ply the Jamaica trade. Since the sacrifice of a single one of these cargo vessels caused terrible losses, merchants yearned to avoid the inevitable. They wished to discover secret routes—and that meant discovering a means to determine longitude.

The pathetic state of navigation alarmed Samuel Pepys, who served for a time as an official of the Royal Navy. Commenting on his 1683 voyage to Tangiers, Pepys wrote: "It is most plain, from the confusion all these people are in, how to make good their reckonings, even each man's with itself, and the nonsensical arguments they would make use of to do it, and disorder they are in about it, that it is by God's Almighty

Providence and great chance, and the wideness of the sea, that there are not a great many more misfortunes and ill chances in navigation than there are."

That passage appeared prescient when the disastrous wreck on the Scillies scuttled four warships. The 1707 incident, so close to the shipping centers of England, catapulted the longitude question into the forefront of national affairs. The sudden loss of so many lives, so many ships, and so much honor all at once, on top of centuries of previous privation, underscored the folly of ocean navigation without a means for finding longitude. The souls of Sir Clowdisley's lost sailors—another two thousand martyrs to the cause—precipitated the famed Longitude Act of 1714, in which Parliament promised a prize of £20,000 for a solution to the longitude problem.

*George Anson (1697-1762) joined the Royal Navy when he was fourteen and within twelve years had become a post captain. When the war with Spain broke out shortly after 1737, he was appointed commodore of a squadron and given orders to disrupt the Spanish trading monopoly across the Pacific Ocean. Following his famous voyage around the world, he was made an admiral and thus became a principal member of the Board of Longitude.*

In 1736, an unknown clockmaker named John Harrison carried a promising possibility on a trial voyage to Lisbon aboard H.M.S. *Centurion.* The ship's officers saw firsthand how Harrison's clock could improve their reckoning. Indeed, they thanked Harrison when his newfangled contraption showed them to be about sixty miles off course on the way home to London.

By September 1740, however, when the *Centurion* set sail for the South Pacific under the command of Commodore George Anson, the longitude clock stood on terra firma in Harrison's house at Red Lion Square. There the inventor, having already completed an improved second version of it, was hard at work on a third with further refinements. But such devices were not yet generally accepted, and would not become generally available for another fifty

*While rounding Cape Horn in March and April 1741, Anson's squadron of seven ships encountered devastating storms. Three of his ships turned back and three others were later wrecked or destroyed by the damage they had sustained. When Anson's crew aboard the* Centurion *sighted Cape Noir, the navigator realized that, on account of the strength of the winds and the current, his estimate of the ship's longitude was about 200 miles in error. As a result of the prolonged voyage, scurvy was claiming the lives of the crew at the rate of about ten men each day. By the time the* Centurion *reached the island of Juan Fernández (today called Isla Robinson Crusoe after the hero of Daniel Defoe's novel of 1719), of the 521 men who had sailed from England only 284 remained.*

years. So Anson's squadron took the Atlantic the old-fashioned way, on the strength of latitude readings, dead reckoning, and good seamanship. The fleet reached Patagonia intact, after an unusually long crossing, but then a grand tragedy unfolded, founded on the loss of their longitude at sea.

On March 7, 1741, with the holds already stinking of scurvy, Anson sailed the *Centurion* through the Straits Le Maire, from the Atlantic into the Pacific Ocean. As he rounded the tip of Cape Horn, a storm blew up from the west. It shredded the sails and pitched the ship so violently that men who lost their holds were dashed to death. The storm abated from time to time only to regather its strength, and punished the *Centurion* for fifty-eight days without mercy. The winds carried rain, sleet, and snow. And scurvy all the while whittled away at the crew, killing six to ten men every day.

Anson held west against this onslaught, more or less along the parallel at sixty degrees south latitude, until he figured he had gone a full two hundred miles westward, beyond Tierra del Fuego. The other five ships of his squadron had been separated from the *Centurion* in the storm, and some of them were lost forever.

On the first moonlit night he had seen in two months, Anson at last anticipated calm waters, and steered north for the earthly paradise called Juan Fernández Island. There he knew he would find fresh water for his men, to soothe the dying and sustain the living. Until then, they would have to survive on hope alone, for several days of sailing on the vast Pacific still separated them from the island oasis. But as the haze cleared, Anson sighted *land* right away, dead ahead. It was Cape Noir, at the western edge of Tierra del Fuego.

*How could this have happened? Had they been sailing in reverse?*

The fierce currents had thwarted Anson. All the time he thought he was gaining westward, he had been virtually treading water. So he had no choice but to head west *again*, then north toward salvation. He knew that if he failed, and if the sailors continued dying at the same rate, there wouldn't be enough hands left to man the rigging.

According to the ship's log, on May 24, 1741, Anson at last delivered the *Centurion* to the latitude of Juan Fernández Island, at thirty-five degrees south. All that remained to do was to run down the parallel to make harbor. But which way should he go? Did the island lie to the east or to the west of the *Centurion*'s present position?

That was anybody's guess.

Anson guessed west, and so headed in that direction. Four more desperate days at sea, however, stripped him of the courage of his conviction, and he turned the ship around.

Forty-eight hours after the *Centurion* began beating east along the thirty-fifth parallel, land was sighted! But it showed itself to be the impermeable, Spanish-ruled, mountain-walled coast of Chile. This jolt required a one-hundred-eighty-degree change in direction, and in Anson's thinking. He was forced to confess that he had probably been within hours of Juan Fernández Island when he abandoned west for east. Once again, the ship had to retrace her course.

On June 9, 1741, the *Centurion* dropped anchor at last at Juan Fernández. The two weeks of zigzag searching for the island had cost Anson an additional eighty lives. Although he was an able navigator who could keep his ship at her proper depth and protect his crew from mass drowning, his delays had given scurvy the upper hand. Anson helped carry the hammocks of sick sailors ashore, then watched helplessly as the scourge picked off his men one by one . . . by one by one, until more than half of the original five hundred were dead and gone.

*The original mission of Anson's voyage was to capture a Spanish treasure galleon. On June 20, 1743, the desperate crew of the* Centurion *sighted the* Nuestra Señora de Cobadonga, *sailing from Acapulco to Manila, and, despite their inferior number, they overwhelmed the Spanish after a short battle. The prize of this galleon amounted to almost £400,000, including 1,313,843 pieces of eight and 35,682 ounces of virgin silver, one of the richest prizes ever captured on the high seas.*

## CHAPTER THREE

# Adrift in a Clockwork Universe

One night I dreamed I was locked in my Father's watch
With Ptolemy and twenty-one ruby stars
Mounted on spheres and the Primum Mobile
Coiled and gleaming to the end of space
And the notched spheres eating each other's rinds
To the last tooth of time, and the case closed.

JOHN CIARDI, "My Father's Watch"

A S ADMIRAL SHOVELL and Commodore Anson showed, even the best sailors lost their bearings once they lost sight of land, for the sea offered no useful clue about longitude. The sky, however, held out hope. Perhaps there was a way to read longitude in the relative positions of the celestial bodies.

The sky turns day to night with a sunset, measures the passing months by the phases of the moon, and marks each season's change with a solstice or an equinox. The rotating, revolving Earth is a cog in a clockwork universe, and people have told time by its motion since time began.

When mariners looked to the heavens for help with navigation, they found a combination compass and clock. The constellations, especially the Little Dipper with the North Star in its handle, showed them where they were going by night—provided, of course, the skies were clear. By day, the sun not only gave direction but also told them the time if they followed its movements. So they watched it rise orange out of the ocean in the east, change to yellow and to blinding white as it gained altitude, until at

*Although not signed or dated, this portrait of Galileo (1564-1642) was probably painted soon after 1610, the year in which he discovered the moons of Jupiter. On January 7, 1610, about a month before his forty-sixth birthday, Galileo observed three tiny bright "stars" extending in a straight line from one side of the planet to the other. By the eleventh, he had concluded that these were moons wandering around the giant planet, like the moon moves around the Earth. On the thirteenth, he observed a fourth moon, and soon after recognized that their regular orbit provided a celestial clock that could be used to solve the longitude problem.*

midday the sun stopped in its tracks—the way a ball tossed in the air pauses momentarily, poised between ascent and descent. That was the noon siren. They set their sandglasses by it every clear day. Now all they needed was some astronomical event to tell them the time somewhere else. If, for example, a total lunar eclipse was predicted for midnight over Madrid, and sailors bound for the West Indies observed it at eleven o'clock at night their time, then they were one hour earlier than Madrid, and therefore fifteen degrees of longitude west of that city.

Solar and lunar eclipses, however, occurred far too rarely to provide any meaningful aid to navigation. With luck, one could hope to get a longitude fix once a year by this technique. Sailors needed an everyday heavenly occurrence.

As early as 1514, the German astronomer Johannes Werner struck on a way to use the motion of the moon as a location finder. The moon travels a distance roughly equal to its own width every hour. At night, it appears to walk through the fields of fixed stars at this stately pace. In the daytime (and the moon is up in the daytime for half of every month) it moves toward or away from the sun.

Werner suggested that astronomers should map the positions of the stars along the moon's path and predict when the moon would brush by each one—on every moonlit night, month to month, for years to come. Also the relative positions of the sun and moon through the daylight hours should be similarly mapped. Astronomers could then publish tables of all the moon's meanderings, with the time of each star meeting predicted for one place—Berlin, perhaps, or Nuremberg—whose longitude would serve as the zero-degree reference point. Armed with such information, a navigator could compare the time he observed the moon near a given star with the time the same conjunction was supposed to occur in the skies over the reference location. He would then determine his longitude by finding the difference in hours between the two places, and multiplying that number by fifteen degrees.

The main problem with this "lunar distance method" was that the positions of the stars, on which the whole process depended, were not at all well known. Then, too, no

INTRODVCTIO

GEOGRAPHICA PETRI APIANI IN DOCTISSIMAS VER-
neri Annotationes, cõtinens plenum intellectum & iudicium omnis operationis, quæ
per sinus & chordas in Geographia confici potest, adiuncto Radio astrono-
mico cum quadrante nouo Meteoroscopii loco longe vtilisimo.

HVIC ACCEDIT Translatio noua primi libri Geographiæ CL, Ptolemæi,
Translationi adiuncta sunt argumenta & paraphrases singulo: capitum: libellus
quo: de quatuor terrarum orbis in plano figurationib: Authore Vernero.

LOCVS etiam pulcherrimus desumptus ex fine septimi libri eiusdem Geographiæ Claudii Ptolemæi de plana terrarum orbis descriptione iam olim & à veterib:
instituta Geographis, vnà cum opusculo Amirucii Constantinopolitani
de iis, quæ Geographiæ debent adesse.

ADIVNCTA est & epistola IOANNIS de Regio monte ad Reuerendissi-
mum patrem & Dominum D, Bessarionem Cardinalem Nicenum, atq: patri-
archam Constantinopolitanum, de compositione & vsu cuiusdam Meteoroscopii armillaris, Cui recens iam opera PETRI APIANI accessit
Torquetum instrumentum pulcherrimũ sane, & vtilisimum.

INGOLSTADII,      Cum Gratia & Priuilegio
Imperiali,           AN, M.D.XXXIII.

This illustration, published by Peter Apian on the title page of his Introductio Geographica of 1533, shows how the cross-staff was used to measure the angular distance of the moon from a star. Apian was one of the most popular and prolific scientific writers of the sixteenth century. His Cosmographicus Liber of 1524, which also describes this "lunar distance method" of finding longitude, was revised and edited by Gemma Frisius in 1529 and had appeared in thirty editions and three languages before 1600.

astronomer could predict exactly where the moon would be from one night or day to the next, since the laws that governed the moon's motion still defied detailed understanding. And besides, sailors had no accurate instruments for measuring moon-to-star distances from a rolling ship. The idea was way ahead of its time. The quest for another cosmic time cue continued.

In 1610, almost one hundred years after Werner's immodest proposal, Galileo Galilei discovered from his balcony in Padua what he thought was the sought-after clock of heaven. As one of the first to turn a telescope to the sky, Galileo encountered an embarrassment of riches there: mountains on the moon, spots on the sun, phases of Venus, a ring around Saturn (which he mistook for a couple of close-set moons), and a family of four satellites orbiting the planet Jupiter the way the planets orbit the sun. Galileo later named these last the Medicean stars. Having thus used the new moons to curry political favor with his Florentine patron, Cosimo de' Medici, he soon saw how they might serve the seaman's cause as well as his own.

Galileo was no sailor, but he knew of the longitude problem—as did every natural philosopher of his day. Over the next year he patiently observed the moons of Jupiter, calculating the orbital periods of these satellites, and counting the number of times the small bodies vanished behind the shadow of the giant in their midst. From the dance of his planetary moons, Galileo worked out a longitude solution. Eclipses of the moons of Jupiter, he claimed, occurred one thousand times annually—and so predictably that one could set a watch by them. He used his observations to create tables of each satellite's expected disappearances and reappearances over the course of several months, and allowed himself dreams of glory, foreseeing the day when whole navies would float on his timetables of astronomical movements, known as ephemerides.

Galileo wrote about his plan to King Philip III of Spain, who was offering a fat life pension in ducats to "the discoverer of longitude." By the time Galileo submitted his scheme to the Spanish court, however, nearly twenty years after the announcement of the prize in 1598, poor Philip had been worn down by crank letters. His staff rejected Galileo's idea on the grounds that sailors would be hard-pressed just to see the satellites

*One of two surviving telescopes attributed to Galileo, this instrument, made of wood covered with paper, is four and a half feet long. Galileo made his first telescope in Padua in August 1609, after hearing news of this Dutch invention. The military advantage of magnifying a sight otherwise invisible to the naked eye was quickly recognized by the Signoria in Venice. Galileo, however, put the instrument to more significant use when he turned it toward the heavens.*

30

Plate IIII.

Fig. I.

Fig. II.

Fig. III.

*J. Fergufon delin.*

*J. Mynde fc.*

from their vessels—and certainly couldn't hope to see them often enough or easily enough to rely on them for navigation. After all, it was never possible to view the hands of the Jupiter clock during daylight hours, when the planet was either absent from the sky or overshadowed by the sun's light. Nighttime observations could be carried on for only part of the year, and then only when skies were clear.

In spite of these obvious difficulties, Galileo had designed a special navigation helmet for finding longitude with the Jovian satellites. The headgear—the *celatone*—has been compared to a brass gas mask in appearance, with a telescope attached to one of the eyeholes. Through the empty eyehole, the observer's naked eye could locate the steady light of Jupiter in the sky. The telescope afforded the other eye a look at the planet's moons.

*Galileo proposed using an eclipse of one of Jupiter's satellites to determine the difference in longitude between two places. The eclipse of the innermost satellite (K behind Jupiter [J]) can be seen at precisely the same moment from points R and Q on Earth (dotted lines T and U). If the observer at Q has tables to compare the time of the eclipse at point R with his local time, he can find the difference in longitude between points R (III [3 A.M.]) and Q (XII [midnight]). This three-hour time difference signifies that Q is forty-five degrees west of point R.*

| Iannuarius. | 1668. |
|---|---|

**Configurationes Mediceorum.**

**Hora 7. P.M.**

*Dies*

| A 1 | 3 ☉ 1 2 4 |
| 2 | ☉ 3 4 |
| 3 | ☉ 4 |
| 4 | ☉ 2 4 3 |
| 5 Primus in facie. | 4 ☉ 3 2 |
| 6 | 4 3 2 ☉ 1 |
| 7 | 4 3 2 1 ☉ |
| A 8 | 4 3 ☉ 2 1 |
| 9 | 4 ☉ 2 3 |
| 10 | 4 2 ☉ 1 3 |
| 11 Secundus poſt ♃ | 4 1 ☉ 3 |
| 12 | 4 ☉ 3 2 |
| 13 Primus poſt ♃ | 3 2 ☉ 4 |
| 14 | 3 2 1 ☉ 4 |
| A 15 | 3 ☉ 1 2 4 |
| 16 Tertius poſt ♃ | 1 ☉ 2 4 |

Con-

*Using a telescope made by the celebrated Italian instrument maker Giuseppe Campani, Giovanni Domenico Cassini calculated tables predicting the positions of Jupiter's satellites as seen from Bologna at 7 P.M. each day of each month for the year 1668. By providing a simple reference by which an observer could predict when an eclipse would take place in Bologna, these tables made Galileo's method practicable for the first time.*

An inveterate experimenter, Galileo took the contraption out on the harbor of Livorno to demonstrate its practicability. He also dispatched one of his students to make test runs aboard a ship, but the method never gained adherents. Galileo himself conceded that, even on land, the pounding of one's heart could cause the whole of Jupiter to jump out of the telescope's field of view.

Nevertheless, Galileo tried to peddle his method to the Tuscan government and to officials in the Netherlands, where other prize money lay unclaimed. He did not collect any of these funds, although the Dutch gave him a gold chain for his efforts at cracking the longitude problem.

Galileo stuck to his moons (now rightly called the Galilean satellites) the rest of his life, following them faithfully until he was too old and too blind to see them any longer. When Galileo died in 1642, interest in the satellites of Jupiter lived on. Galileo's method for finding longitude at last became generally accepted after 1650—but only on land. Surveyors and cartographers used Galileo's technique to redraw the world. And it was in the arena of mapmaking that the ability to determine longitude won its first great victory. Earlier maps had underestimated the distances to other continents and exaggerated the outlines of individual nations. Now global dimensions could be set, with authority, by the celestial spheres. Indeed, King Louis XIV of France, confronted with a revised map of his domain based on accurate longitude measurements, reportedly complained that he was losing more territory to his astronomers than to his enemies.

The success of Galileo's method had mapmakers clamoring for further refinements in predicting eclipses of the Jovian satellites. Greater precision in the timing of these events would permit greater exactitude in charting. With the borders of kingdoms hanging in the balance, numerous astronomers found gainful employment observing the moons and improving the accuracy of the printed tables. In 1668, Giovanni Domenico Cassini, a professor of astronomy at the University of Bologna, published the best set yet, based on the most numerous and most carefully conducted observations. Cassini's well-wrought ephemerides won him an invitation to Paris to the court of the Sun King.

*Giovanni Domenico (Jean-Dominique) Cassini (1625-1712) made a number of important contributions to astronomy. His published tables predicting the times of the eclipses of Jupiter's satellites brought Cassini to the attention of the French minister, Jean Baptiste Colbert, who invited him to the Académie Royale des Sciences in Paris. Cassini subsequently became director of the newly constructed Paris Observatory.*

Louis XIV, despite any disgruntlement about his diminishing domain, showed a soft spot for science. He had given his blessing to the founding, in 1666, of the French Académie Royale des Sciences, the brainchild of his chief minister, Jean Colbert. Also at Colbert's urging, and under the ever-increasing pressure to solve the longitude problem, King Louis approved the building of an astronomical observatory in Paris. Colbert then lured famous foreign scientists to France to fill the ranks of the Académie and man the observatory. He imported Christiaan Huygens as charter member of the former, and Cassini as director of the latter. (Huygens went home to Holland eventually and traveled several times to England in relation to his work on longitude, but Cassini grew roots in France and never left. Having become a French citizen in 1673, he is remembered as a French astronomer, so that his name today is given as Jean-Dominique as often as Giovanni Domenico.)

From his post at the new observatory, Cassini sent envoys to Denmark, to the ruins of Uranienborg, the "heavenly castle" built by Tycho Brahe, the greatest naked-eye astronomer of all time. Using observations of Jupiter's satellites taken at these two sites, Paris and Uranienborg, Cassini confirmed the latitude and longitude of both. Cassini also called on observers in Poland and Germany to cooperate in an international task force devoted to longitude measurements, as gauged by the motions of Jupiter's moons.

ANGLETERRE

L'OCEAN

CARTE DE
FRANCE
*Corrigée par Ordre
du Roy sur les Observations
de M. de l'Academie
des sciences*

LA MANCHE

FLANDRE

PICARDIE

PARALLELE DE PARIS

OCCI:

NORMANDIE

PARIS

BRETAGNE

DENTAL

MER

DE

POITOU

DE PARIS

GASCOGNE

ITALIE

MERIDIEN

GASCOGNE

LANGUEDOC

PROVENCE

ESPAGNE

*This map of the coastline of
France shows two seventeenth-
century delineations
superimposed on a computer-
generated projection. The
survey published in 1693
(shaded line) was based on
observations of Jupiter's
satellites and shows a marked
improvement in accuracy over
the former survey of 1679 (fine
line), particularly in the
determination of the longitude.*

It was during this ferment of activity at the Paris Observatory that visiting Danish astronomer Ole Roemer made a startling discovery: The eclipses of all four Jovian satellites would occur ahead of schedule when the Earth came closest to Jupiter in its orbit around the sun. Similarly, the eclipses fell behind the predicted schedules by several minutes when the Earth moved farthest from Jupiter. Roemer concluded, correctly, that the explanation lay in the velocity of light. The eclipses surely occurred with sidereal regularity, as astronomers claimed. But the time that those eclipses could be observed on Earth depended on the distance that the light from Jupiter's moons had to travel across space.

Until this realization, light was thought to get from place to place in a twinkling, with no finite velocity that could be measured by man. Roemer now recognized that earlier attempts to clock the speed of light had failed because the distances tested were

OPPOSITE *Louis XIV and
his minister Jean Baptiste
Colbert visit the Académie
Royale des Sciences. The Paris
Observatory is visible in the
distance through the window.*

RIGHT *The Paris Observatory was founded by Louis XIV in 1667 and became the prime meridian from which the new French surveys were measured.*

BELOW *Ole Roemer (1644-1710) studied astronomy and mathematics at the University of Copenhagen. In 1671, he accompanied the French astronomer Jean Picard to Tycho Brahe's observatory on the island of Hven, where they made observations of the eclipses of Jupiter's satellites in order to establish its precise location. Picard persuaded Roemer to go with him to Paris, and Roemer remained there for the next nine years. In 1676, after observing that the eclipses of Jupiter's satellites were consistently retarded at certain times of the year, he deduced that light had a finite velocity. In 1681, he returned to Denmark, where he became astronomer royal and director of the Copenhagen observatory.*

too short. Galileo, for example, had tried in vain to time a light signal traveling from a lantern on one Italian hilltop to an observer on another. He never detected any difference in speed, no matter how far apart the hills he and his assistants climbed. But in Roemer's present, albeit inadvertent, experiment, Earthbound astronomers were watching for the light of a moon to reemerge from the shadow of another world. Across these immense interplanetary distances, significant differences in the arrival times of light signals showed up. Roemer used the departures from predicted eclipse times to measure the speed of light for the first time in 1676. (He slightly underestimated the accepted modern value of approximately 300,000 kilometers per second.)

ABOVE *In this diagram explaining how Roemer determined the velocity of light, J represents Jupiter and CBADH the orbit of the Earth around the sun (S). The distance AB (one-sixth of the Earth's orbit, about sixty-one days) equals SA, the distance from the sun to the Earth, which was estimated in the 1670s to be about 92 million miles. Having observed that the eclipse of the innermost satellite at point 1 occurred about eleven minutes sooner when the Earth was at point B than when it was at point A in its orbit, Roemer determined that light has a finite velocity and calculated that it travels 92 million miles in eleven minutes, or about 140,000 miles per second. The current accepted value is 186,282 miles (299,792 km.) per second.*

LEFT *Dressed in gown and hat to keep warm during a long, cold night of observing at his house in Copenhagen, Roemer is using his transit instrument —a telescope with a fixed mounting that he invented —to determine the exact moment a star or planet crossed his meridian. He timed these observations precisely, using the pendulum clock on the wall. This is the type of long-pendulum clock designed and used by Christiaan Huygens.*

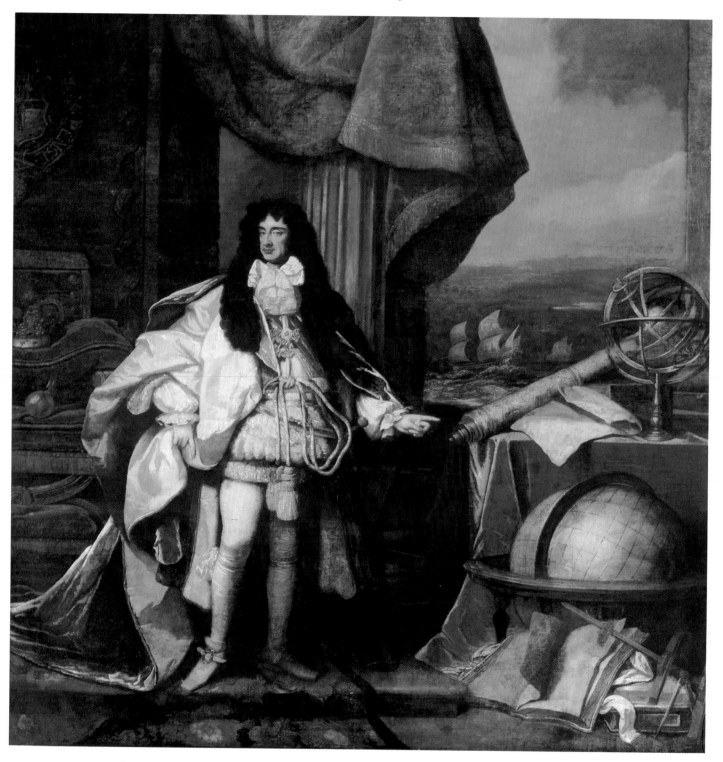

In England, by this time, a royal commission was embarked on a wild goose chase — a feasibility study of finding longitude by the dip of the magnetic compass needle on seagoing vessels. King Charles II, head of the largest merchant fleet in the world, felt the urgency of the longitude problem acutely, and desperately hoped the solution would sprout from his soil. Charles must have been pleased when his mistress, a young Frenchwoman named Louise de Kéroualle, reported this bit of news: One of her countrymen had arrived at a method for finding longitude and had himself recently arrived from across the Channel to request an audience with His Majesty. Charles agreed to hear the man out.

The Frenchman, the sieur de St. Pierre, frowned on the moons of Jupiter as a means of determining longitude, though they were all the rage in Paris. He put his personal faith in the guiding powers of Earth's moon, he said. He proposed to find longitude by the position of the moon and some select stars — much as Johannes Werner had suggested one hundred sixty years previously. The king found the idea intriguing, so he redirected the efforts of his royal commissioners, who included Robert Hooke, a polymath equally at home behind a telescope or a microscope, and Christopher Wren, architect of St. Paul's Cathedral.

For the appraisal of St. Pierre's theory, the commissioners called in the expert testimony of John Flamsteed, a twenty-seven-year-old astronomer. Flamsteed's report judged the method to be sound in theory but impractical in the extreme. Although some passing fair observing instruments had been developed over the years, thanks to Galileo's influence, there was still no good map of the stars and no known route for the moon.

Flamsteed, with youth and pluck on his side, suggested that the king might remedy this situation by establishing an observatory with a staff to carry out the necessary work. The king complied. He also appointed Flamsteed his first personal "astronomical observator" — a title later changed to astronomer royal. In his warrant establishing the Observatory at Greenwich, the king charged Flamsteed to apply "the most exact Care and Diligence to rectifying the Tables of the Motions of the Heavens, and the Places of

OPPOSITE *Charles II (1630-85) was proclaimed king of England in 1660. He provided considerable encouragement and support for the sciences, establishing the Royal Society in 1662 and the Royal Observatory in 1675. This painting of about 1670 reveals his interest in astronomy and navigation.*

BELOW *This portrait of John Flamsteed (1646-1719) was painted soon after he became the first astronomer royal in 1675. On an annual stipend of only £100, he was unable to afford his own instruments, most of which were provided by his patron, Sir Jonas Moore. To supplement his income, he took private pupils, and, as an ordained minister, he was granted the living from a small church in Surrey in 1684. The continual lack of financial support from the government caused Flamsteed to regard the results of his observations as his own property. After his death, his widow removed all of his instruments from the Observatory.*

The Royal Observatory at Greenwich in 1676, shown here from the southeast in a view looking toward London, was built in 1675. A royal warrant stipulated its purpose was to perfect astronomy and navigation, and authorized an expenditure of £500 for the purpose. The cost, which in fact came to £520 9s. 10., was covered by the sale of old, decayed gunpowder.

LONDINUM.

the fixed Stars, so as to find out the so-much desired Longitude at Sea, for perfecting the art of Navigation."

In Flamsteed's own later account of the turn of these events, he wrote that King Charles "certainly did not want his ship-owners and sailors to be deprived of any help the Heavens could supply, whereby navigation could be made safer."

Thus the founding philosophy of the Royal Observatory, like that of the Paris Observatory before it, viewed astronomy as a means to an end. All the far-flung stars must be cataloged, so as to chart a course for sailors over the oceans of the Earth.

Commissioner Wren executed the design of the Royal Observatory. He set it, as the king's charter decreed, on the highest ground in Greenwich Park, complete with lodging rooms for Flamsteed and one assistant. Commissioner Hooke directed the actual building work, which got under way in July of 1675 and consumed the better part of one year.

Flamsteed took up residence the following May (in a building still called Flamsteed House today) and collected enough instruments to get to work in earnest by October. He toiled at his task for more than four decades. The excellent star catalog he compiled was published posthumously in 1725. By then, Sir Isaac Newton had begun to subdue the confusion over the moon's motion with his theory of gravitation. This progress bolstered the dream that the heavens would one day reveal longitude.

Meanwhile, far from the hilltop haunts of astronomers, craftsmen and clockmakers pursued an alternate path to a longitude solution. According to one hopeful dream of ideal navigation, the ship's captain learned his longitude in the comfort of his cabin, by comparing his pocket watch to a constant clock that told him the correct time at home port.

*The Royal Observatory's "Camera Stellata" (Star Chamber), now called the Octagon Room, was used for observing comets, occultations of stars by the moon, and eclipses of the sun, the moon, and Jupiter's satellites. The telescopes and other instruments were moved from window to window as needed, and observations were timed by the clocks.*

PROSPECTUS INTRA CAMERAM STELLATAM.

Qui varium coeli morem penitusq̃
remoti
Mortales docuit ætheris
ire vias:
Quiq̃ nouos Medicis meditando
repperit vsus,
Hęc Gemæ effigies, hic fuit
oris honos.

## CHAPTER FOUR

# Time in a Bottle

There being no mystic communion of clocks
        it hardly matters when this autumn breeze
        wheeled down from the sun
        to make leaves skirt pavement like a
        million lemmings.

An event is such a little piece of time-and-space
        you can mail it through the slotted eye of a cat.

DIANE ACKERMAN, "Mystic Communion of Clocks"

TIME IS TO CLOCK as mind is to brain. The clock or watch somehow contains the time. And yet time refuses to be bottled up like a genie stuffed in a lamp. Whether it flows as sand or turns on wheels within wheels, time escapes irretrievably, while we watch. Even when the bulbs of the hourglass shatter, when darkness withholds the shadow from the sundial, when the mainspring winds down so far that the clock hands hold still as death, time itself keeps on. The most we can hope a watch to do is mark that progress. And since time sets its own tempo, like a heartbeat or an ebb tide, timepieces don't really keep time. They just keep up with it, if they're able.

Some clock enthusiasts suspected that good timekeepers might suffice to solve the longitude problem, by enabling mariners to carry the home-port time aboard ship with them, like a barrel of water or a side of beef. Starting in 1530, Flemish astronomer Gemma Frisius hailed the mechanical clock as a contender in the effort to find longitude at sea.

*Gemma Frisius (1508-55) proposed the idea of using a mechanical timekeeper for finding longitude in 1530, when he was twenty-two years old. In the right foreground of this portrait (which was engraved in 1557, two years after he died) is a universal ring dial, an ingenious device that he invented about 1552 for finding local time at sea.*

*Small, portable, mechanical timekeepers like the one shown here were in use at the time that Gemma Frisius suggested his method of finding longitude. They were usually suspended from a cord attached to a belt or worn around the neck; the drum shape of this example, about two inches in diameter, would have been inconvenient to carry, but in any case these timekeepers were far too unreliable and inaccurate to be of use for navigational purposes.*

"In our times we have seen the appearance of various small clocks, capably constructed, which, for their modest dimensions, provide no problem to those who travel," Frisius wrote. He must have meant they provided no problem of heft or high price to rich travelers; certainly they did not keep time very well. "And it is with their help that the longitude can be found." The two conditions that Frisius spelled out, however—namely, that the clock be set to the hour of departure with "the greatest exactness" and that it not be allowed to run down during the voyage—virtually ruled out any chance of applying the method at that time. The clocks of the early sixteenth century weren't equal to the task. They were neither accurate nor able to run true against the assault of changing temperature on the high seas.

Although it is not clear whether he knew of Gemma Frisius's suggestion, William Cunningham of England revived the timekeeper idea in 1559, recommending watches "such as are brought from Flanders" or found "without Temple barre," right in London, for the purpose. But these watches typically gained or lost as many as fifteen minutes a day, and thus fell far short of the accuracy required to determine one's whereabouts. (Multiplying a difference in hours by fifteen degrees gives only an approximation of location; one also needs to divide the number of minutes and seconds by four, to convert the time readings to degrees and minutes of arc.) Nor had timepieces enjoyed any significant advances by 1622, when English navigator Thomas Blundeville proposed using "some true Horologie or Watch" to determine longitude on transoceanic voyages.

The shortcomings of the watch, however, failed to squelch the dream of what it might do once perfected.

Galileo, who, as a young medical student, successfully applied a pendulum to the problem of taking pulses, late in life hatched plans for the first pendulum clock. In June of 1637, according to Galileo's protégé and biographer, Vincenzo Viviani, the great man described his idea for adapting the pendulum "to clocks with wheelwork for assisting the navigator to determine his longitude."

Legends of Galileo recount an early mystical experience in church that fostered his profound insights about the pendulum as timekeeper: Mesmerized by the to-and-fro of an oil lamp suspended from the nave ceiling and pushed by drafts, he watched as the sexton stopped the pan to light the wick. Rekindled and released with a shove, the chandelier began to swing again, describing a larger arc this time. Timing the motion of the lamp by his own pulse, Galileo saw that the length of a pendulum determines its rate.

Galileo always intended to put this remarkable observation to work in a pendulum clock, but he never got around to building one. His son, Vincenzio, constructed a model from Galileo's drawings, and the city fathers of Florence later built a tower clock predicated on that design. However, the distinction for completing the first working pendulum clock fell to Galileo's intellectual heir, Christiaan Huygens, the landed son of a Dutch diplomat who made science his life.

Huygens, also a gifted astronomer, had divined that the "moons" Galileo observed at Saturn were really a *ring*, impossible as that seemed at the time. Huygens also discovered Saturn's largest moon, which he named Titan, and was the first to notice markings on Mars. But Huygens couldn't be tied to the telescope all the time. He had too many other things on his mind. It is even said that he chided Cassini, his boss at the Paris Observatory, for the director's slavish devotion to daily observing.

*This pencil drawing of Galileo's pendulum-controlled mechanism was made in 1659 by or for Galileo's pupil, Vincenzo Viviani. It reveals Galileo's idea for using a pendulum and the design of his ingenious escapement, but no provision has been made either for a power source or for a dial. An incomplete iron model recorded at the time of Galileo's son's death in 1649 has not survived.*

Christiaan Huygens (1629-95) was one of the leading astronomers and mathematicians of the seventeenth century. At the age of twenty-six, having devised a new method to grind and polish lenses, he made a telescope with which he discovered the first satellite of Saturn and recognized the correct form of its ring. In the following year, he invented the pendulum clock, which resulted in his subsequent studies of the cycloid. The importance of his work was quickly recognized throughout Europe. He was elected a Fellow of the newly founded Royal Society in 1663 and became a member of the Académie Royale des Sciences in 1666, the year it was established.

Huygens, best known as the first great horologist, swore he arrived at the idea for the pendulum clock independently of Galileo. And indeed he evinced a deeper understanding of the physics of pendulum swings—and the problem of keeping them going at a constant rate—when he developed his first pendulum-regulated clock in 1656. Two years later Huygens published a treatise on its principles, called the *Horologium*, in which he declared his clock a fit instrument for establishing longitude at sea.

By 1660, Huygens had completed not one but two marine timekeepers based on his principles. He tested them carefully over the next several years, sending them off with cooperative sea captains. On the third such trial, in 1664, Huygens's clocks sailed to the Cape Verde Islands, in the North Atlantic off the west coast of Africa, and kept good track of the ship's longitude all the way there and back.

ABOVE *Huygens produced this sketch to describe to his friend Jean Chapelain in Paris how he transformed his balance-controlled timekeeper into a pendulum-controlled timekeeper and thereby, on December 25, 1656, invented the first pendulum clock.*

LEFT *This detail shows the movement of one of Huygens's first pendulum clocks, made in 1657 by Salomon Coster in The Hague. The two curved pieces of brass on either side of the pendulum's suspension were intended to guide the pendulum in a cycloidal rather than a circular arc, so that each oscillation, regardless of its amplitude, would take the same period of time. Although Huygens perfected the theory of cycloidal cheeks, there were several factors that affected the success of his idea in practice. When the problem was overcome by the invention of a new escapement that substantially reduced the required arc of oscillation, the use of cycloidal cheeks died out. In the 1720s, however, John Harrison designed adjustable cycloidal cheeks and used them with great success in his precision longcase clocks.*

*Huygens published this drawing of his proposed clock for finding longitude at sea in his* Horologium Oscillatorium *of 1673, a book he dedicated to Louis XIV. The clock is mounted in gimbals and has a triangular pendulum about six and a quarter inches long suspended from cycloidal cheeks. The dial, which Huygens had introduced in the 1660s and became the standard design used for astronomical clocks, has separate rings for indicating the hours, minutes, and seconds. Despite numerous attempts, Huygens was unable to overcome the difficulties of making a reliable and accurate marine timekeeper. As a result, many (including Isaac Newton) thought that the longitude problem would never be solved with a clock.*

Now a recognized authority on the subject, Huygens published another book in 1665, the *Kort Onderwys*, his directions for the use of marine timekeepers. Subsequent voyages, however, exposed a certain finickiness in these machines. They seemed to require favorable weather to perform faithfully. The swaying of the ship on a storm's waves confounded the normal swinging of the pendulum.

To circumvent this problem, Huygens invented the spiral balance spring as an alternative to the pendulum for setting a clock's rate, and had it patented in France in 1675. Once again, Huygens found himself under pressure to prove himself the inventor of a new advance in timekeeping, when he met a hot-blooded and headstrong competitor in the person of Robert Hooke.

Hooke had already made several memorable names for himself in science. As a biologist studying the microscopic structure of insect parts, bird feathers, and fish scales, he applied the word *cell* to describe the tiny chambers he discerned in living forms. Hooke was also a surveyor and builder who helped reconstruct the city of London after the great fire of 1666. As a physicist, Hooke had his hand in fathoming the behavior of light, the theory of gravity, the feasibility of steam engines, the cause of earthquakes, and the action of springs. Here, in the coiled contrivance of the balance spring, Hooke clashed with Huygens, claiming the Dutchman had stolen his concept.

The Hooke-Huygens conflict over the right to an English patent for the spiral balance spring disrupted several meetings of the Royal Society, and eventually the matter was dropped from the minutes, without being decided to either contestant's satisfaction.

In the end, there was no end to the strife, though neither Hooke nor Huygens produced a true marine timekeeper. The separate failures of these two giants seemed to dampen the prospects for ever solving the longitude problem with a clock. Disdainful astronomers, still struggling to amass the necessary data required to employ their lunar distance technique, leaped at the chance to renounce the timekeeper approach. As far as they could see, the answer would come from the heavens—from the clockwork universe and not from any ordinary clock.

ABOVE *Robert Hooke (1635-1703), shown here in a modern portrait based on contemporary descriptions, was appointed curator of experiments to the Royal Society in 1662. He was ingenious, but jealousy often brought him into conflict with anyone who made a discovery or invention in one of the many fields in which he was engaged.*

LEFT *Huygens's earliest sketch of a balance spring to control the motion of the balance in a watch was made in Paris on January 20, 1675. Before applying for a patent, he went, on January 22, to see Isaac Thuret, the best maker in Paris at the time, to have a model made. While putting the idea into practice, Thuret introduced several improvements and made an additional model for himself, for which he applied for his own patent. Huygens was deeply distressed by this breach of confidence, but the revised sketch he made a day later reveals improvements he evidently obtained from Thuret to make the invention practicable.*

Will:<sup>m</sup> Whiston
A. M.

## CHAPTER FIVE

# Powder of Sympathy

The College will the whole world measure;
Which most impossible conclude,
And Navigation make a pleasure
By finding out the Longitude.
Every Tarpaulin shall then with ease
Sayle any ship to the Antipodes.

ANONYMOUS (ABOUT 1660) "Ballad of Gresham College"

A T THE END OF THE seventeenth century, even as members of learned societies debated the means to a longitude solution, countless cranks and opportunists published pamphlets to promulgate their own harebrained schemes for finding longitude at sea.

Surely the most colorful of the offbeat approaches was the wounded dog theory, put forth in 1687. It was predicated on a quack cure called powder of sympathy. This miraculous powder, discovered in southern France by the dashing Sir Kenelm Digby, could purportedly heal at a distance. All one had to do to unleash its magic was to apply it to an article from the ailing person. A bit of bandage from a wound, for example, when sprinkled with powder of sympathy, would hasten the closing of that wound. Unfortunately, the cure was not painless, and Sir Kenelm was rumored to have made his patients jump by powdering—for medicinal purposes—the knives that had cut them, or by dipping their dressings into a solution of the powder.

*William Whiston (1667-1752), a graduate and Fellow of Clare College, Cambridge, became Isaac Newton's assistant lecturer in mathematics in 1701 and succeeded him as Lucasian professor in 1703. He lost this appointment seven years later, however, on account of his fervent religious views. After moving to London, he worked with Humphry Ditton (1675-1715) of Christ's Hospital on several schemes to solve the longitude problem. Although failing to win the longitude prize, through persistence and boundless energy he was awarded £500 in 1741 to survey the chief ports and coasts of Great Britain.*

A LATE
## DISCOURSE

Made in a Solemne Assembly
of Nobles and Learned
Men at *Montpellier*
in *France*;

By Sr. *Kenelme Digby*, Knight,&c.

Touching the Cure of W O U N D S
by the *Powder of Sympathy*; With
Inſtruƈtions how to make the
ſaid Powder; whereby many
other Secrets of Nature
are unfolded.

*Fælix qui potuit* Rerum *cognoſcere*
cauſas.

Rendred faithfully out of French
into Engliſh

By R. *White*, *Gent.*

London, Printed for R. *Lownes*, and
*T. Davies*, and are to be ſold at their ſhops in
Sr. Pauls Church yard, at the ſign of the *White
Lion*, and at the *Bible* over againſt the little
North Door of St. Pauls Church, 1658.

*In the first English edition of his lecture of 1658 given in Montpellier, France, Sir Kenelm Digby described a powder that could cure wounds at a distance. Twenty-nine years later, some witty writer suggested using Digby's powder to solve the longitude problem.*

The daft idea to apply Digby's powder to the longitude problem follows naturally enough to the prepared mind: Send aboard a wounded dog as a ship sets sail. Leave ashore a trusted individual to dip the dog's bandage into the sympathy solution every day at noon. The dog would perforce yelp in reaction, and thereby provide the captain a time cue. The dog's cry would mean, "the Sun is upon the Meridian in London." The captain could then compare that hour to the local time on ship and figure the longitude accordingly. One had to hope, of course, that the powder really held the power to be felt many thousand leagues over the sea, and yet—and this is very important—fail to heal the telltale wound over the course of several months. (Some historians suggest that the dog might have had to be injured more than once on a major voyage.)

Whether this longitude solution was intended as science or satire, the author points out that submitting "a Dog to the misery of having always a Wound about him" is no more macabre or mercenary than expecting a seaman to put out his own eye for the purposes of navigation. "[B]efore the Back-Quadrants were Invented," the pamphlet states, "when the Forestaff was most in use, there was not one Old Master of a Ship amongst Twenty, but what a Blind in one Eye by daily staring in the Sun to find his Way." This was true enough. When English navigator and explorer John Davis introduced the backstaff in 1595, sailors immediately hailed it as a great improvement over the old cross-staff, or Jacob's staff. The original sighting sticks had required them to measure the height of the sun above the horizon by looking directly into its glare, with only scant eye protection afforded by the darkened bits of glass on the instruments' sighting holes. A few years of such observations were enough to destroy anyone's eyesight. Yet the observations had to be made. And after all those early navigators lost at least half their vision finding the latitude, who would wince at wounding a few wretched dogs in the quest for longitude?

Sir Kenelm Digby (1603-65) was an English diplomat, a devout Catholic, and a staunch royalist who escaped to France during the English Civil War. Despite his claims for the "Powder of Sympathy," which no doubt originated from his interest in astrology and alchemy, he became one of the original members of the Royal Society and is said to have been the first to explain the necessity of oxygen to the life of plants.

# CROSS-STAFF AND BACKSTAFF

RIGHT The cross-staff was first described by the Jewish astronomer Levi ben Gerson in 1330 and was subsequently developed into various specialized designs for use in astronomy, surveying, and navigation. The model developed for navigation employed four separate sighting vanes, each one paired with a scale on the four-sided staff. This illustration of 1594

shows a navigator determining latitude by observing the altitude of the Pole Star. Prolonged use of this instrument was painful and damaging to the eye, but, although superseded by better instruments, the cross-staff remained in use into the nineteenth century, because it was inexpensive.

LEFT In 1595, Captain John Davis published a book showing two designs for a new instrument that could be used to measure the altitude of the sun. Davis's design allowed the navigator to make this observation with his back to the sun, thereby overcoming one of the inherent faults of the cross-staff, which required the observer to face the sun. Davis's quadrant, which became known as the backstaff, was rapidly adopted by mariners, but its accuracy in determining latitude was limited to about one-sixth of a degree.

A much more humane solution lay in the magnetic compass, which had been invented in the twelfth century and become standard equipment on all ships by this time. Mounted on gimbals, so that it remained upright regardless of the ship's position, and kept inside a binnacle, a stand that supported it and protected it from the elements, the compass helped sailors find direction when overcast skies obscured the sun by day or the North Star at night. But the combination of a clear night sky and a good compass *together*, many seamen believed, could also tell a ship's longitude. For if a navigator could read the compass and see the stars, he could get his longitude by splitting the distance between the two north poles—the magnetic and the true.

The compass needle points to the magnetic north pole. The North Star, however, hovers above the actual pole—or close to it. As a ship sails east or west along any given parallel in the northern hemisphere, the navigator can note how the distance between the magnetic and the true pole changes: At certain meridians in the mid-Atlantic the

*The azimuth, or variation, compass was invented in the sixteenth century to determine the difference between true north, found by observing the position of the sun or stars through the sights, and magnetic north, indicated by the compass needle. This example, made by the London maker Edward Nairne, was sold to Harvard College in August 1765 for £5 15s. 6d.*

intervening distance looks large, while from certain Pacific vantage points the two poles seem to overlap. (To make a model of this phenomenon, stick a whole clove into a navel orange, about an inch from the navel, and then rotate the orange slowly at eye level.) A chart could be drawn—and many were—linking longitude to the observable distance between magnetic north and true north.

This so-called magnetic variation method had one distinct advantage over all the astronomical approaches: It did not depend on knowing the time at two places at once or knowing when a predicted event would occur. No time differences had to be established or subtracted from one another or multiplied by any number of degrees. The relative positions of the magnetic pole and the Pole Star sufficed to give a longitude reading in degrees east or west. The method seemingly answered the dream of laying legible longitude lines on the surface of the globe, except that it was incomplete and inaccurate. Rare was the compass needle that pointed precisely north at all times; most displayed some degree of variation, and even the variation varied from one voyage to the next, making it tough to get precise measurements. What's more, the results were further contaminated by the vagaries of terrestrial magnetism, the strength of which waxed or waned with time in different regions of the seas, as Edmond Halley found during a two-year voyage of observation.

In 1699, Samuel Fyler, the seventy-year-old rector of Stockton, in Wiltshire, England, came up with a way to draw longitude meridians on the night sky. He figured that he—or someone else more versed in astronomy—could identify discrete rows of stars, rising from the horizon to the apex of the heavens. There should be twenty-four of these star-spangled meridians, or one for each hour of the day. Then it would be a simple matter, Fyler supposed, to prepare a map and timetable stating when each line would be visible over the Canary Islands, where the prime meridian lay by convention in those days. The sailor could observe the row of stars above his head at local midnight. If it were the fourth, for argument's sake, and his tables told him the first row should be over the Canaries just then, assuming he had some knowledge of the time, he

OPPOSITE *Edmond Halley published this isogonic chart of the Atlantic in 1701, after his voyage to the South Seas in the* Paramore. *The lines marking various degrees of magnetic variation cross the lines of latitude and therefore provide, in theory, the two coordinates required to determine the location of a ship at sea. The amount of magnetic variation shown by the variation compass would determine one coordinate, while the latitude, found by measuring the height of the sun at noon, established the other. In practice, however, it was discovered that the Earth's magnetic fields change over time, and all attempts to predict the variation of the variation failed.*

*57*

LONGITUDINIS
Inventæ Explicatio
NON LONGA,
O R,
Fixing the VOLATILIS'D,
AND TAKING
TIME ON TIPTOE,
Briefly Explain'd;

By which Rules are given to find the Longitude at Sea by, as truly and exactly as the Latitude is found by the Star in the Tayle of Urſa Minor, call'd the Pole-Star.

Nauta Sciens, modò fiⁱVigilans, dominabitur Aſtris.

By S. F. A. M. Rector of Stockton in the County of Wilts.

LONDON, Printed for the Author, in the Year, 1699.

In addition to mapping out twenty-four imaginary meridians of longitude in the sky, Samuel Fyler's proposal for solving the longitude problem involved "quick and speedy observation in finding agen those stars," which he termed "taking Time on Tiptoe."

could figure his longitude as three hours—or forty-five degrees—west of those islands. Even on a clear night, however, Fyler's approach invoked more astronomical data than existed in all the world's observatories, and its reasoning was as circular as the celestial sphere.

Admiral Shovell's disastrous multishipwreck on the Scilly Isles after the turn of the eighteenth century intensified the pressure to solve the longitude problem.

Two infamous entrants into the fray in the aftermath of this accident were William Whiston and Humphry Ditton, mathematicians and friends, who often engaged each other in wide-ranging discussions. Whiston had already succeeded his mentor, Isaac Newton, as Lucasian professor of mathematics at Cambridge—and then lost the post on account of his unorthodox religious views, such as his natural explanation for Noah's flood. Ditton served as master of the mathematics school at Christ's Hospital, London. In a long afternoon of pleasant conversation, this pair hit on a scheme for solving the longitude problem.

As they later reconstructed the train of their thought in print, Mr. Ditton reasoned that sounds might serve as a signal to seamen. Cannon reports or other very loud noises, intentionally sounded at certain times from known reference points, could fill the oceans with audible landmarks. Mr. Whiston, concurring heartily, recalled that the blasts of the great guns fired in the engagement with the French fleet off Beachy Head, in Sussex, had reached his own ears in Cambridge, some ninety miles away. And he had also learned, on good authority, that explosions from the artillery of the Dutch Wars carried to "the very middle of *England*, at a much greater distance."

If enough signal boats, therefore, were stationed at strategic points from sea to sea, sailors could gauge their distance from these stationary gun ships by comparing the known time of the expected signal to the actual shipboard time when the signal was heard. In so doing, providing they factored in the speed of propagation of sound, they would discover their longitude.

Unfortunately, when the men offered their brainchild to seafarers, they were told that sounds would not carry at sea reliably enough for accurate location finding. The plan might well have died then, had not Whiston hit on the idea of combining sound and light. If the proposed signal guns were loaded with cannon shells that shot more than a mile high into the air, and exploded there, sailors could time the delay between seeing the fireball and hearing its big bang—much the way the weather wise gauge the distance of electrical storms by counting the seconds elapsed between a flash of lightning and a clap of thunder.

Whiston worried, of course, that bright lights might also falter when trying to deliver a time signal at sea. Thus he took special delight in watching the fireworks display commemorating the Thanksgiving Day for the Peace, on July 7, 1713. It convinced him that a well-timed bomb, exploding 6,440 feet in the air, which he figured was the limit of available technology, could certainly be seen from a distance of 100 miles. Thus assured, he worked with Ditton on an article that appeared the following week in *The Guardian*, laying out the necessary steps.

First a new breed of fleet must be dispatched and anchored at 600-mile intervals in the oceans. Whiston and Ditton didn't see any problem here, as they misjudged the length requirements for anchor chains. They stated the depth of the North Atlantic as 300 fathoms at its deepest point, when in fact the average depth is more like 2,000 fathoms, and the sea bottom occasionally dips down to more than 3,450.

Where waters were too deep for anchors to hold, the authors said, weights could be dropped through the currents to calmer realms, and would serve to immobilize the ships. In any case, they were confident these minor bugs could be worked out through trial and error.

A meatier matter was the determination of each hull's position. The time signals must originate from places of known latitude and longitude. Eclipses of the moons of

Jupiter could be used for this operation—or even solar or lunar eclipses, since the determinations need not be made with any great frequency. The lunar distance method, too, might serve to locate these hulls, and spare passing ships the difficult astronomical observations and tedious calculations.

All the navigator had to do was watch for the signal flare at local midnight, listen for the cannon's roar, and sail on, confident of the ship's position between fixed points at sea. If clouds got in the way, obscuring the flash, then the sound would have to suffice. And besides, another fix on location would come soon from another hull.

*In the hope of winning the £20,000 prize, William Whiston and Humphry Ditton in 1714 published this pamphlet of finding longitude at sea. Their method, shown in the explanatory diagram on the right, was totally impractical at the time.*

---

*A. Paul*

A

# New METHOD

For Difcovering the

# LONGITUDE

BOTH AT

# SEA and LAND,

Humbly Propofed to the Confideration
of the PUBLICK.

---

B Y

| | | |
|---|---|---|
| *William Whifton*, M. A. fometime Profeffor of the Mathematicks in the Univerfity of Cambridg. | and | *Humphry Ditton*, Mafter of the New Mathematick School in *Chrift's Hofpital*, London. |

---

*L O N D O N :*

Printed for JOHN PHILLIPS, at the *Black Bull* in Cornhill. 1714. *July 15.*

---

32    *A new Method*

This appears by the Demonſtration following.   Let the Proportion of the Velocity of the Wind, to the Velocity of the Motion of the Air that caufes the Sound, be as A B to A D.

Let the two equal Circles G D H E, G C H F, be defcribed upon the Centers A and B; and let any Line, as K L, be drawn Parallel to D F. K I will therefore be always equal to M L.

The hulls, the authors hoped, would be naturally exempt from all acts of piracy or attack by warring states. Indeed, they should receive legal protection from all trading nations: "And it ought to be a great Crime with every one of them, if any other Ships either injure them, or endeavor to imitate their Explosions, for the Amusement and Deception of any."

Critics were quick to point out that even if all the obvious obstacles could be overcome, not the least of which was the expense of such an undertaking, many more problems would still stand in the way. A cast of thousands would be required to man the hulls. And these men would be worse off than lighthouse keepers—lonely, at the mercy of the elements, possibly threatened by starvation, and hard pressed to stay sober.

On December 10, 1713, the Whiston-Ditton proposal was published a second time, in *The Englishman*. In 1714 it came out in book form, under the title *A New Method for Discovering the Longitude both at Sea and Land*. Despite their scheme's insurmountable shortcomings, Whiston and Ditton succeeded in pushing the longitude crisis to its resolution. By dint of their dogged determination and desire for public recognition, they united the shipping interests in London. In the spring of 1714, they got up a petition signed by "Captains of Her Majesty's Ships, Merchants of London, and Commanders of Merchant-Men." This document, like a gauntlet thrown down on the floor of Parliament, demanded that the government pay attention to the longitude problem—and hasten the day when longitude should cease to be a problem—by offering rich rewards to anyone who could find longitude at sea accurately and practicably.

The merchants and seamen called for a committee to consider the current state of affairs. They requested a fund to support research and development of promising ideas. And they demanded a king's ransom for the author of the true solution.

EDMVND. HALLEIVS LL.D.
GEOM. PROF. SAVIL. & R.S. SECRET.

## CHAPTER SIX

# The Prize

Her cutty sark, o' Paisley harn,
That while a lassie she had worn,
In longitude tho' sorely scanty,
It was her best, and she was vauntie.

ROBERT BURNS, "Tam o' Shanter"

THE MERCHANTS' AND SEAMEN'S petition pressing for action on the matter of longitude arrived at Westminster Palace in May of 1714. In June, a Parliamentary committee assembled to respond to its challenge.

Under orders to act quickly, the committee members sought expert advice from Sir Isaac Newton, by then a grand old man of seventy-two, and his friend Edmond Halley. Halley had gone to the island of St. Helena some years earlier to map the stars of the southern hemisphere—virtually virgin territory on the landscape of the night. Halley's published catalog of more than three hundred southern stars had won him election to the Royal Society. He had also traveled far and wide to measure magnetic variation, so he was well versed in longitude lore—and personally immersed in the quest.

Newton prepared written remarks for the committee members, which he read aloud to them, and also answered their questions, despite his "mental fatigue" that day. He summarized the existing means for determining longitude, saying that all of them were true in theory but "difficult to execute." This was of course a gross understatement. Here, for example, is Newton's description of the timekeeper approach:

*Edmond Halley (c. 1656-1742) had a long and distinguished career, being elected a Fellow of the Royal Society in 1678, when he was twenty-two, and serving as astronomer royal from 1720 until his death in 1742. Although he became a proponent of the lunar distance method, he had the foresight to recognize that it was not necessarily the only solution to the longitude problem. In 1730, he gave sound advice to John Harrison by encouraging him to visit the famous London clockmaker George Graham and later, as a member of the Board of Longitude, offered Harrison his influential support. This portrait was probably painted soon after 1687.*

"One [method] is by a Watch to keep time exactly. But, by reason of the motion of the Ship, the Variation of Heat and Cold, Wet and Dry, and the Difference of Gravity in different Latitudes, such a watch hath not yet been made." And not likely to be, either, he implied.

Perhaps Newton mentioned the watch first so as to set it up as a straw man, before proceeding to the somewhat more promising though still problematic field of astronomical solutions. He mentioned the eclipses of Jupiter's satellites, which worked on land, at any rate, though they left mariners in the lurch. Other astronomical methods, he said, counted on the predicted disappearances of known stars behind our

*Isaac Newton (1642-1727) was the most influential scientist of his day. After he finished school in Lincolnshire, his mother thought that he should become a farmer, but through encouragement from his uncle and his teacher, he went to Trinity College, Cambridge, in 1661. At twenty-six, he was appointed Lucasian Professor of Mathematics and began preparing his greatest work, the* Principia, *which was published in London in 1687. Newton became convinced that the lunar distance method was the only practicable solution to the longitude problem, but even he was unable to solve the problem of predicting the moon's motion. He did not believe that a clock of sufficient accuracy and reliability would ever be made. After the Longitude Act was passed in 1714, all the far-fetched proposals were referred to him.*

356    Anno Regni duodecimo Annæ Reginæ.

own moon, or on the timed observations of lunar and solar eclipses. He also cited the grandiose "lunar distance" plan for divining longitude by measuring the distance between the moon and sun by day, between the moon and stars at night. (Even as Newton spoke, Flamsteed was giving himself a migraine at the Royal Observatory, trying to ascertain stellar positions as the basis for this much-vaunted method.)

The longitude committee incorporated Newton's testimony in its official report. The document did not favor one approach over another, or even British genius over foreign ingenuity. It simply urged Parliament to welcome potential solutions from any field of science or art, put forth by individuals or groups of any nationality, and to reward success handsomely.

LEFT *Although not the first reward offered for a solution to the longitude problem, the Act of Queen Anne, 12, cap. 15 (the Longitude Act), passed on July 8, 1714, provided by far the largest incentive.*

RIGHT *The passage at the bottom of the second page of the 1714 Longitude Act details the three levels of reward offered for a successful solution to the problem of finding longitude at sea.*

65

The actual Longitude Act, issued in the reign of Queen Anne on July 8, 1714, did all these things. On the subject of prize money, it named first-, second-, and third-prize amounts, as follows:

> £20,000 for a method to determine longitude to an accuracy of half a degree of a great circle;
> £15,000 for a method accurate to within two-thirds of a degree;
> £10,000 for a method accurate to within one degree.

Since one degree of longitude spans sixty nautical miles (the equivalent of sixty-eight geographical miles) over the surface of the globe at the Equator, even a fraction of a degree translates into a large distance—and consequently a great margin of error when trying to determine the whereabouts of a ship vis-à-vis its destination. The fact that the government was willing to award such huge sums for "Practicable and Useful" methods that could miss the mark by many miles eloquently expresses the nation's desperation over navigation's sorry state.

The Longitude Act established a blue ribbon panel of judges that became known as the Board of Longitude. This board, which consisted of scientists, naval officers, and government officials, exercised discretion over the distribution of the prize money. The astronomer royal served as an ex officio member, as did the president of the Royal Society, the first lord of the Admiralty, the speaker of the House of Commons, the first commissioner of the Navy, and the Savilian, Lucasian, and Plumian professors of mathematics at Oxford and Cambridge Universities. (Newton, a Cambridge man, had held the Lucasian professorship for thirty years; in 1714 he was president of the Royal Society.)

The board, according to the Longitude Act, could give incentive awards to help impoverished inventors bring promising ideas to fruition. This power over purse strings made the Board of Longitude perhaps the world's first official research-and-development agency. (Though none could have foreseen it at the outset, the Board of

Longitude was to remain in existence for more than one hundred years. By the time it finally disbanded in 1828, it had disbursed funds in excess of £100,000.)

In order for the commissioners of longitude to judge the actual accuracy of any proposal, the technique had to be tested on one of Her Majesty's ships, as it sailed "over the ocean, from Great Britain to any such Port in the West Indies as those Commissioners Choose ... without losing their Longitude beyond the limits before mentioned."

So-called solutions to the longitude problem had been a dime a dozen even before the act went into effect. After 1714, with their potential value exponentially raised, such schemes proliferated. In time, the board was literally besieged by any number of conniving and well-meaning persons who had heard word of the prize and wanted to win it. Some of these hopeful contenders were so galvanized by greed that they never stopped to consider the conditions of the contest. Thus the board received ideas for improving ships' rudders, for purifying drinking water at sea, and for perfecting special sails to be used in storms. Over the course of its long history, the board received all too many blueprints for perpetual motion machines and proposals that purported to square the circle or make sense of the value of pi.

In the wake of the Longitude Act, the concept of "discovering the longitude" became a synonym for attempting the impossible. Longitude came up so commonly as a topic of conversation—and the butt of jokes—that it rooted itself in the literature of the age. In *Gulliver's Travels*, for example, the good Captain Lemuel Gulliver, when asked to imagine himself as an immortal Struldbrugg, anticipates the enjoyment of witnessing the return of various comets, the lessening of mighty rivers into shallow brooks, and "the discovery of the *longitude*, the *perpetual motion*, the *universal medicine*, and many other great inventions brought to the utmost perfection."

Part of the sport of tackling the longitude problem entailed ridiculing others in the competition. A pamphleteer who signed himself "R.B." said of Mr. Whiston, the fireball proponent, "[I]f he has any such Thing as Brains, they are really crackt."

## JANE SQUIRE

A

# PROPOSAL

To Determine our

# LONGITUDE.

BY

## *JANE SQUIRE.*

---

The Second Edition, in English only.

---

---

### *LONDON:*

Printed for the AUTHOR, and fold by S. Cope, at the *Bible*, in *King-Street* near *Golden-Square*; and by the Bookfellers of *London* and *Weft-minfter.* 1743.

The £20,000 prize attracted so many nonsensical solutions to the longitude problem that the proponents were labeled "longitudinarians." Jane Squire, the only woman to offer a solution, wouldn't take no for an answer and had sufficient social standing to harangue the Board of Longitude for ten years. Failing to convince the astronomer royal, Edmond Halley, of the soundness of her proposal, she went after the Speaker of the House of Commons and then the first lord of the Admiralty, both of whom managed to evade involvement. Recognizing that members of the Royal Society were avoiding her, she jumped to the conclusion that her idea had been stolen when the eminent clockmaker George Graham presented his sidereal clock to the Board of Longitude. Her proposal, printed in 1731, was published in a second, enlarged edition in 1743.

Jane Squire's proposal for solving the longitude problem involved dividing the sky into more than 1.25 million "cloves," or numbered spaces, which anyone intended for the sea should learn by heart. Equipped with an "astral" (sidereal time) watch, a navigator only had to recognize the clove directly overhead in order to calculate his longitude from Squire's prime meridian, which ran through the manger at Bethlehem.

# LODGITUDE

*Si consideratur, Satis;*      *Si non consideratur, nimis;*

## NAMES & Characters of NUMBERS

| Ba | 1 |
| Ca | 2 |
| Da | 3 |
| Ea | 4 |
| Fa | 5 |
| Gaa | 6 |
| Ra | 7 |
| Ja | 8 |
| Da | 9 |
| Ma | 10 |
| Ma | 100 |
| Mama | 1000 |
| Mama | 1,000,000 |

The Numerators to D, C, M, & Mam.

| a | one |
| e | two |
| i | three |
| o | four |
| u | five |
| ua | six |
| ui | seven |
| uo | eight |
| no | nine |

*Sometimes as here in particular Names of Measure & Weights*

Characters expressing Numbers

Other Characters expressing:
- Addition
- Subtraction
- Multiplication
- Division
- Equality
- Number
- Weight
- Measure
- Time
- Place or Space
- A Line
- A Square
- A Cube
- A Cylinder
- A Circle
- A Sphere on Card
- A Cube
- A Diagonal
- A Wind
- An Axis
- A Pole
- Nota bene
- H Pecet
- Remainder

## GIVING

GIVING, in Absolute Measure, (Regulated by the Degree of the Equator proposed to be adjusted by Astronomical Observations & measured by a Water Wheel, (made of Matter not subject to Rust, Rot, or Wear out soon) & other Wheels; All giving the number of their Rotations upon a Plane, like a Dial Plate) the exact Place of every part of Space & Quantity of Matter: expressed in numerical Names & Characters; distinguishing 13 several Denominations of Lines (when absolute & entire) always consisting of 60 Cubes of the next lower Denomination, Squares of 3600, & Cubes of 216,000 (when otherways) distinguished by the numerical Vowels following their Denominations; & the addition of la, de, di, do, du (each containing its proper Cylinder, Circle or Sphere &c. From the Cedamuagrae (or Infinitum the Aedamuagrae) &c) to the Seculae (or even to the Agacedamia) is intended to reduce the whole useful Sciences of counting & measuring, to plain & clear, 1, 2, 3, & every distinct Cube of a determined Matter, is a determined Weight; & by Weight to determine the Square of the Circle &c.

---

| General Names & Characters for Measures | The particular Names & Characters proper to Lines | S Squares | C Cubes | O Cylinders | So Circles | Co Spheres | Cocardas A Sphere divided into Clover, Rings & Cards |
|---|---|---|---|---|---|---|---|
| G G | | Asquar & or | Asquar & or | Asquar & or | Asquar & So | Asquar & Co | Acards Acards |
| Cedamuagra | Cedamuagra | Cedamuagras | Cedamuagris | Cedamuagrao | Cedamuagraso | Cedamuagraco | Cedamuagracocal |
| M G Micuagra | Micuagra | | | | | | |
| G G Diagra | Diagra | | | | | | |
| G Degree | Gra | | | | | | |
| V Mile | Vi | | | | | | |
| X Lene | Xa | | | | | | |
| Z Min | Za | | | | | | |
| & Mindua | Eta | | | | | | |
| I Pin | Ja | | | | | | |
| J Pindua | Ja | | | | | | |
| H Nin | Ha | | | | | | |
| R Nindua | Ra | | | | | | |
| Sl Ninnicua | Scala | | | | | | |

*Scala Salvator Hominum Ramator Secula Seculorum*

---

### The Relative Measure

The Relative Measure proper to a Sphere (counting, & counted by Time: the giving that of the Day; the Sun, that of the Year; & the precession of the Equinox being supposed, or rather that the Suns course is a precessive Spiral) the Year current, by the comparing of which, with absolute measure we may determine the form & dimension of the Earth; And after, by comparing absolute Measure, with the Relative found proper to the Sun, we may discover our Longitude. For as the same absolute measure can only measure a Clove, &c. in the same Ring of Latitude, upon a Sphere of a determined Size & form, the same absolute Time (or Minute &c. of the Astrol Day) can only give Noon, or any determined Solar Time, to a determined Clove &c. of Longitude.

| Gen'l Names & Characters | Wth Charac of the particulars | Seconds, Thirds &c. proper to the Degree of a Circle | Faa Equaaza | | Caa Equaaa | |
|---|---|---|---|---|---|---|
| Cubes of Longitude | Ba | Seconds, Thirds &c. proper to the Hour or Degree in Time | Faata | | Caata | |
| | | | Equaaruda | | Equaaruda | |
| Ring of Latitude | Timba | | | | | |
| Card, or 1st of a Day in Long & Lat | Ba Timba | | | | | |
| Astral Minute | Bati Equaaruda | | | | | |
| Astral Hour | Scala Equagruda | | | | | |
| Astral Day | Bar | | | | | |
| Solar Day | Solbar | | | | | |
| Lunar Day | Lunbar | | | | | |
| A Year | Rosecasona | | | | | |
| The Suns Lonsitudional Year | Solsen | | | | | |
| The Suns Longitudional Year | Solona | | | | | |
| The Moons Latitudional Year | Lubata | | | | | |
| The Moons Longitudional year | Lulona | | | | | |
| The Moons great Year | Lulolata | | | | | |
| The Solar Month | Solsna | | | | | |
| The Calend, Mth? | Luna | | | | | |

As God has given us no other regular perpetual Motion but of Revolution of the Firmament, or revolving Sphere; & only can count Astral Time, of Days Minutes &c. of 60, are always of the same length.

A first Celestial & first Terrestial Meridian being fixt upon, Astrol Days will all begin & end & count their several Minutes at the same instant of Time, all over the World.

If this first Terrestial Meridian, be that on which we find Bethlehem & the first Celestial one that which cuts the Equator, between Gemini and Cancer, our Astrol Time may be counted in Days, Minutes &c. of our Solar as in Years, Month, Days &c. from the Birth of our Lord Christ, the number of Revolutions made by the Heavens since giving a Name to each Astrol Day, as the Number of Cloves, first Cedastial Meridian, is departed from a first terrestial one, to the several Minutes in it.

Clocks & Watches made to give this Astrol Time in regular Beats, each Beat giving a Second a Third or rather a certain number of Thirds, as suppose 12 &c. gives 18,000 Beats in an Hour, must be of best help, nor can have to count any Time by, for as they represent a regular motion, we are quit of the impossibility to ever must attend the attempt of giving our unequatical Solar Time by any Instrument of that kind; & having the constant Revolution of Heavens, at all times & in all places to correct it by; they must have many advantages if all such as are made to give our imaginary Equated Solar Time.

The Sun & Moon & Solar time, given by Dials &c. give us nice use the particular Instruments for a purpose, but a little turn, & a little Moon moveable at pleasure, on the Dial Plate of an Astrol Watch or Clock, may enable us to mark the Astrol Time when the Sun, or Moon, & when Moon comes to the Meridian where we are, & at what Astrol Time the same happens the Day before. By this always seeing the Excess of the preceding Solar Day above the Astrol we have an infallibly proof of the correctness; or an exact correction of our Equation Tables &c. we may by it in Astrol Time give Solar Lunar or any other Time, the first only being absolute determined & always the same (having probably by the Lights being placed in one consequential of the Revolving Firmament when first divided from darkness) Lighted as well as counted the great Days, before the Sun & Moon were created; the new ones, God has made the Sun to Rule over Day & the Moon to Rule over Night, the Light of the Day & by the Face of the whole Heavens becoming all sprinkled over with Stars (of different Magnitudes) divided into Minutes, as they may be found between the Meridians supposed to divide the Heavens into 1440 equal parts, all distinguishable from each other by the different numbers & disposition of the Stars upon them, giving in them the 1440 several Minutes of the Astrol Day & in it an exact measure for Time.

Thus the Sun & Moon since their Creation Rule every Day, & the motion of the Firmament, does so alter, that time, by the different Phenomenon of the fixe stars, in every part; of it, counts of different length of each, whilst the Planets (who like the undoubtedly Created by God, for Us the Children of Adam) seem (at least to me) to be given us at another time, for another purpose, quite foreign to what was here intended to be spoke of; which was number & Weight, chiefly as they regard Measure and Measure, as it regards Time.

The Precession of the Equinox, can only be adjusted by astrol Observation & in the giving of Long; & then gives Noon when it is upon the Meridian compared with it Plate, it gives Noon, to return on it Equator at the last Equinox, of one same Denomination.

Dec. 25, 1732.

Gladwin-aidena

J. Squire

---

## PARTS of LODGITUDE with the proper length

| Lth Blew | Longitude |
| Ld Yellow | Latitude |
| Ld Red | Longitude |
| Lth Green Purple and Flame colour | Locitude |
| Ld Brown | Lodigitude |
| Dth White | Dacuigitude |
| Cth Black | Conuirgitude |

Every Sphere is here supposed to have a fixt Meridian upon its left hand side; from whence it counts 1440 Cloves of Longitude, all equally divided by Meridian Lines; & the Rings of Lat. on each side to Equator at right angles, divides its Surface into 1,036,800. Cards

Tax North, or the Top

Tax South, or the Bottom

Ata East, or the Righthand

Ita West, or Left Hand

In the E. & W. sides of the 360 &c 360 S Rings of Latitude &c the diagonal & Round Lines represent the Number of the Compound Diagonals of Squares Cubes & Cones &c.

The Sun &c is here presenting only its Circular radiation upon a Surface of Spheres; & represents the Section in a solid Sphere, being distinguished by T, as Cube in absolute Measure &c & So, expressing of universal radiations into Cona Elipses & Spheroids.

A Cylinder, Circle or Sphere radiated into the contain Triangulos or Triangular Figures, is equal to a Square Ola Sola Cola &c. If the sides be unequal, the Points of the compound radial of each Angle may describe them, if irregular, they must be consider'd as placed in a square or in a Cube.

being always expressed by a Matter must consequence by Day or Night, shall be judged to proper & placed on all the 4 sides of the square Pate, but to ease the N on Land should exactly face the E.

W N. & South.

THE

# LONGITUDES

### EXAMIN'D.

Beginning with a fhort Epiftle to the

*Longitudinarians,*

AND

Ending with the Defcription of a fmart, pretty

# MACHINE

*Of my Own,*

Which I am (almoft) fure will do for
the LONGITUDE, and procure me
THE

## Twenty Thoufand Pounds.

By JEREMY THACKER,
Of *Beverley* in *Yorkfhire.*

*——— Quid non mortalia pectora cogis*
*Auri facra Fames !* ———

### LONDON:

Printed for J. ROBERTS, at the *Oxford-Arms*
in *Warwick-Lane.* 1714. Price 6 *d.*

Surely one of the most astute, succinct dismissals of fellow hopefuls came from the pen of Jeremy Thacker of Beverly, England. Having heard the half-baked bids to find longitude in the sound of cannon blasts, in compass needles heated by fire, in the moon's motion, in the sun's elevation, and what-else-have-you, Thacker developed a new clock ensconced in a vacuum chamber and declared it the best method of all: "In a word, I am satisfied that my Reader begins to think that the *Phonometers, Pyrometers, Selenometers, Heliometers,* and all the *Meters* are not worthy to be compared with my *Chronometer."*

Thacker's witty neologism is apparently the first coinage of the word *chronometer.* What he said in 1714, perhaps in jest, later gained acceptance as the perfect moniker for the marine timekeeper. We still call such a device a chronometer today. Thacker's chronometer, however, was not quite as good as its name. To its credit, the clock boasted two important new advances. One was its glass house—the vacuum chamber that shielded the chronometer from troubling changes of atmospheric pressure and humidity. The other was a set of cleverly paired winding rods, configured so as to keep the machine going while being wound up. Until Thacker's introduction of this "maintaining power," spring-driven watches had simply stopped and lost track of time during winding. Thacker had also taken the precaution of suspending the whole machine in gimbals, like a ship's compass, to keep it from thumping about on a storm-tossed deck.

What Thacker's watch could *not* do was adjust to changes in temperature. Although the vacuum chamber provided some insulation against the effects of heat and cold, it fell short of perfection, and Thacker knew it.

Room temperature exerted a powerful influence on the going rate of any timekeeper. Metal pendulum rods expanded with heat, contracted when cooled, and beat out seconds at different tempos, depending on the temperature. Similarly, balance springs grew soft and weak when heated, stiffer and stronger when cooled. Thacker

*Fig. 4.*

OPPOSITE *Jeremy Thacker described his machine for finding longitude at sea in this pamphlet, which was published toward the end of 1714. It was considerably more practical than some of the preposterous ideas suggested by his contemporaries, and Thacker wasted no time in pointing this out: "I should take Mr. W—n [Whiston] and Mr. D—n [Ditton] in Hand, shipwreck their Hulls, drown their Sounds in a Tempest, lift up the Waves to intercept the Sight of their Fires, and break their General Peace; but Gratitude forbids; They sprung the Twenty Thousand Pounds, and as I hope to get it, I ought to be civil to them."*

LEFT *Thacker's "chronometer" from his pamphlet* The Longitudes Examin'd, *shown here suspended in its gimbals, was highly original in several respects, not least that it was housed in an evacuated jar. Thacker produced a table showing the clock's rate at different temperatures, so that its variation due to temperature change could be predicted. Nevertheless, as ingenious as it must have been, the machine could not have lived up to its maker's expectations, because it was never heard of again. Thacker, however, made his mark in history by being the first to use the word* chronometer *in print, although the term did not come into general use until after 1780.*

had considered this problem at great length when testing his chronometer. In fact, the proposal he submitted to the longitude board contained his careful records of the chronometer's rate at various temperature readings, along with a sliding scale showing the range of error that could be expected at different temperatures. A mariner using the chronometer would simply have to weigh the time shown on the clock's dial against the height of the mercury in the thermometer tube, and make the necessary calculations. This is where the plan falls apart: Someone would have to keep constant watch over the chronometer, noting all changes in ambient temperature and figuring them into the longitude reading. Then, too, even under ideal circumstances, Thacker owned that his chronometer occasionally erred by as many as six seconds a day.

Six seconds sound like nothing compared to the fifteen minutes routinely lost by earlier clocks. Why split hairs?

Because of the consequences—and the money—involved.

To prove worthy of the £20,000 prize, a clock had to find longitude within half a degree. This meant that it could not lose or gain more than three seconds in twenty-four hours. Arithmetic makes the point: Half a degree of longitude equals two minutes of time—the maximum allowable mistake over the course of a six-week voyage from England to the Caribbean. An error of only three seconds a day, compounded every day at sea for forty days, adds up to two minutes by journey's end.

Thacker's pamphlet, the best of the lot reviewed by members of the Board of Longitude during their first year, didn't raise anyone's hopes very high. So much remained to be done. And so little had actually been accomplished.

Newton grew impatient. It was clear to him now that any hope of settling the longitude matter lay in the stars. The lunar distance method that had been proposed several times over preceding centuries gained credence and adherents as the science of astronomy improved. Thanks to Newton's own efforts in formulating the Universal Law of Gravitation, the moon's motion was better understood and to some extent predictable. Yet the world was still waiting on Flamsteed to finish surveying the stars.

Flamsteed, meticulous to a fault, had spent forty years mapping the heavens—and had still not released his data. He kept it all under seal at Greenwich. Newton and Halley managed to get hold of most of Flamsteed's records from the Royal Observatory, and published their own pirated edition of his star catalog in 1712. Flamsteed retaliated by collecting three hundred of the four hundred printed copies, and burning them.

"I committed them to the fire about a fortnight ago," Flamsteed wrote to his former observing assistant Abraham Sharp. "If Sir I. N. would be sensible of it, I have done both him and Dr. Halley a very great kindness." In other words, the published positions, insufficiently verified as they were, could only discredit a respectable astronomer's reputation.

Despite the flap over the premature star catalog, Newton continued to believe that the regular motions of the clockwork universe would prevail in guiding ships at sea. A man-made clock would certainly prove a useful accessory to astronomical reckoning but could never stand in its stead. After seven years of service on the Board of Longitude, in 1721, Newton wrote these impressions in a letter to Josiah Burchett, the secretary of the Admiralty:

"A good watch may serve to keep a recconing at Sea for some days and to know the time of a celestial Observ[at]ion: and for this end a good Jewel watch may suffice till a better sort of Watch can be found out. But when the Longitude at sea is once lost, it cannot be found again by any watch."

Newton died in 1727, and therefore did not live to see the great longitude prize awarded at last, four decades later, to the self-educated maker of an oversized pocket watch.

## CHAPTER SEVEN

# Cogmaker's Journal

Oh! She was perfect, past all parallel—
    Of any modern female saint's comparison;
So far above the cunning powers of hell,
    Her guardian angel had given up his garrison;
Even her minutest motions went as well
    As those of the best time-piece made by Harrison.

LORD BYRON, "Don Juan"

SO LITTLE IS KNOWN of the early life of John Harrison that his biographers have had to spin the few thin facts into whole cloth.

These highlights, however, recall such stirring elements in the lives of other legendary men that they give Harrison's story a leg up. For instance, Harrison educated himself with the same hunger for knowledge that kept young Abraham Lincoln reading through the night by candlelight. He went from, if not rags, then assuredly humble beginnings to riches by virtue of his own inventiveness and diligence, in the manner of Thomas Edison or Benjamin Franklin. And, at the risk of overstretching the metaphor, Harrison started out as a carpenter, spending the first thirty years of his life in virtual anonymity before his ideas began to attract the world's attention.

John "Longitude" Harrison was born March 24, 1693, in the county of Yorkshire, the eldest of five children. His family, in keeping with the custom of the time, dealt out names so parsimoniously that it is impossible to keep track of all the Henrys, Johns, and Elizabeths without pencil and paper. To wit, John Harrison served as the son,

*This movement belongs to John Harrison's first longcase clock, completed in 1713 when he was twenty. Because Harrison was trained as a joiner, he modified the standard design of a grandfather clock movement so that it could be constructed of wood, largely oak and boxwood. Brass and steel were used only where necessary, the former for the escape wheel and the bearings (set into the plates), and the latter for the pivots and the escapement. The clock, which struck every hour, was wound by removing the spandrels beneath the dial and inserting a geared winding key, which meshed with a gear mounted on the winding barrel.*

OPPOSITE *John Harrison was born in Foulby near Wakefield, Yorkshire, and was baptized on March 31, 1693. His father was a carpenter, probably employed on the nearby estate, Nostell Priory (see "Foleby" and "Nostal Priory" on top inset map). Around 1700, the family moved forty-two miles due east to the small village of Barrow upon Humber in Lincolnshire, three miles from the market town of Barton upon Humber, which, by the post road shown on this 1730 map, was 161 miles north of London. Hull, the third largest seaport in England at that time, is situated about four miles north of Barrow, across the River Humber.*

grandson, brother, and uncle of one Henry Harrison or another, while his mother, his sister, both his wives, his only daughter, and two of his three daughters-in-law all answered to the name Elizabeth.

His first home seems to have been on the estate, called Nostell Priory, of a rich landowner who employed the elder Harrison as a carpenter and custodian. Early in John's life—perhaps around his fourth birthday, not later than his seventh—the family moved, for reasons unknown, forty-two miles away to the small Lincolnshire village of Barrow, also called Barrow upon Humber because it sat on the south bank of that river.

In Barrow, young John learned woodworking from his father. No one knows where he learned music, but he played the viol, rang and tuned the church bells, and eventually took over as choirmaster at the Barrow parish church. (Many years later, as an adjunct to the 1775 publication explaining his timekeepers, *A Description Concerning Such Mechanism . . .* , Harrison would expound his radical theory on the musical scale.)

Somehow, John as a teenager let it be known that he craved book learning. He may have said as much aloud, or perhaps his fascination for the way things work burned in his eyes so brightly that others could see it. In any case, in about 1712, a clergyman visiting the parish encouraged John's curiosity by letting him borrow a treasured textbook—a manuscript copy of a lecture series on natural philosophy delivered by mathematician Nicholas Saunderson at Cambridge University.

By the time this book reached his hands, John Harrison had already mastered reading and writing. He applied both skills to Saunderson's work, making his own annotated copy, which he headed "Mr. Saunderson's Mechanicks." He wrote out every word and drew and labeled every diagram, the better to understand the nature of the laws of motion. He pored over this copybook again and again, in the manner of a biblical scholar, continuing to add his own marginal notes and later insights over the next several years. The handwriting throughout appears neat and small and regular, as one might expect from a man of methodical mind.

*John Harrison's transcript of one of Professor Nicholas Saunderson's lectures offers a fragment of evidence of how Harrison gained his sophisticated knowledge of mechanics. This illustration was taken from the 1921 Sotheran catalogue, in which this and other significant documents relating to his life and work were advertised for sale. The buyer of these lots has not been traced, and the present whereabouts of the items is unknown.*

Although John Harrison forswore Shakespeare, never allowing the Bard's works in his house, Newton's *Principia* and Saunderson's lectures stood him in good stead for the rest of his life, strengthening his own firm grasp on the natural world.

Harrison completed his first pendulum clock in 1713, before he was twenty years old. Why he chose to take on this project and how he excelled at it with no experience as a watchmaker's apprentice, remain mysteries. Yet the clock itself remains. Its movement and dial—signed, dated fossils from that formative period—now occupy an exhibit case at The Worshipful Company of Clockmakers' one-room museum at Guildhall in London.

Aside from the fact that the great John Harrison built it, the clock claims uniqueness for another singular feature: It is constructed almost entirely of wood. This is a carpenter's clock, with oak wheels and boxwood axles connected and impelled by small amounts of brass and steel. Harrison, ever practical and resourceful, took what materials came to hand, and handled them well. The wooden teeth of the wheels never snapped off with normal wear but defied destruction by their design, which let them draw strength from the grain pattern of the mighty oak.

Historians wonder which clocks, if any, Harrison might have dismantled and studied before fashioning his own. A tale, probably apocryphal, holds that he sustained himself through a childhood illness by listening to the ticking of a pocket watch laid upon his pillow. But no one can guess where the boy would have gotten such a thing. Clocks and watches carried high price tags in Harrison's youth.

Harrison built two more, almost identical, wooden clocks in 1715 and 1717. In the centuries since their completion, the pendulums and tall cases of these time machines

*This clock was completed by John Harrison in 1715. The gold leaf applied to the wooden dial plate (left) gave it the appearance of brass, conforming to the traditional style of that period, and helped to conceal the fact that the clock was made of wood. The oak plates supporting the wheels of the movement (right) are fastened into the oak frame with brass latches. Like the two identical examples he made in 1713 and 1717, this clock indicates the hour, the minute, and the date. These clocks were signed and dated on the paper covering their wooden date wheels.*

*This table, which John Harrison calculated for his 1717 clock, indicates the "equation of time," the number of minutes and seconds that must be added or subtracted when setting the clock to time with a sundial. While clocks maintain an equal measure of time (mean time) throughout the year, solar time is subject to a cycle of gaining and losing, because the Earth is tilted on its axis and orbits the sun in an elliptical path. Only four times each year are sun time and clock time the same. The discrepancy is known as the equation of time.*

have vanished, so that only the hearts of the works come down to us. The exception is a single piece, roughly the size of a legal document, from the wooden door of the last of the trio. In fact, an actual document, pasted to the door's inside surface, seems to have preserved the soft wood for posterity. This protective paper, Harrison's "equation of time" table, can be seen today in the same Guildhall exhibit case as his first clock.

The table enabled the clock's user to rectify the difference between solar, or "true" time (as shown on a sundial) with the artificial but more regular "mean" time (as measured by clocks that strike noon every twenty-four hours). The disparity between solar noon and mean noon widens and narrows as the seasons change, on a sliding scale. We take no note of solar time today, relying solely on Greenwich mean time as our standard, but in Harrison's era sundials still enjoyed wide use. A good mechanical clock had to be reckoned with the clockwork universe, and this was done through the application of some mathematical legerdemain called the equation of time. Harrison not only understood these calculations in his youth but also made his own astronomical observations and worked out the equation data by himself.

Summarizing the essence of his conversion chart in a handwritten heading, Harrison called it "A Table of the Sun rising and Setting in the Latitude of Barrow 53 degrees 18 Minutes; also of difference that should & will be betwixt ye Longpendillom & ye Sun if ye Clock go true." This description owes its quaint sound partly to its antiquity, and partly to ambiguity. Harrison, according to those who admired him most, never could express himself clearly in writing. He wrote with the scrivener's equivalent of marbles in the mouth. No matter how brilliantly ideas formed in his mind, or crystallized in his clockworks, his verbal descriptions failed to shine with the same light. His last published work, which outlines the whole history of his unsavory dealings with the Board of Longitude, brings his style of endless circumlocution to its peak. The first sentence runs on, virtually unpunctuated, for twenty-five pages.

Forthright in his personal encounters, Harrison proposed marriage to Elizabeth Barrel, and she became his wife on August 30, 1718. Their son, John, was born the following summer. Then Elizabeth fell ill and died in the spring before the boy turned seven.

The dearth of detail regarding the widower's private life at this juncture comes as no surprise, for he left no diaries or letters describing his activities or his angst. Nevertheless, the parish records show that he found a new bride, ten years younger, within six months of Elizabeth's death. Harrison wed his second wife, Elizabeth Scott, on November 23, 1726. At the start of their fifty years together they had two children—William, born in 1728, who was to become his father's champion and right-hand man, and Elizabeth, born in 1732, about whom nothing is known save the date of her baptism, December 21. John, the child of Harrison's first marriage, died when he was only eighteen.

No one knows when or how Harrison first heard word of the longitude prize. Some say that the nearby port of Hull, just five miles north of Harrison's home and the third largest port in England, would have been abuzz with the news. From there, any seaman or merchant could have carried the announcement downstream across the Humber on the ferry.

One would imagine that Harrison grew up well aware of the longitude problem— just as any alert schoolchild nowadays knows that cancer cries out for a cure and that there's no good way to get rid of nuclear waste. Longitude posed the great technological challenge of Harrison's age. He seems to have begun thinking of a way to tell time and longitude at sea even before Parliament promised any reward for doing so—or at least before he learned of the posted reward. In any case, whether or not his thoughts favored longitude, Harrison kept busy with tasks that prepared his mind to solve the problem.

Brocklesby Park, an estate about nine miles south of Barrow upon Humber, was rebuilt in the early years of the eighteenth century, and the stables were constructed around 1720. The stable clock, which Harrison designed and made around 1722, appears from the outside to be an ordinary tower clock, but its wooden movement represents Harrison's first attempt to overcome friction at the outset of his quest for precision timekeeping.

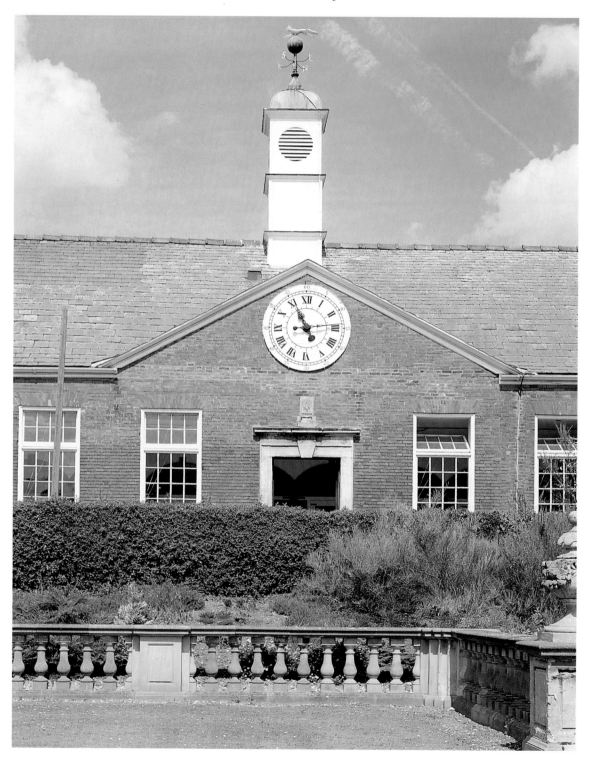

Sometime around 1720, after Harrison had acquired something of a local reputation as a clockmaker, Sir Charles Pelham hired him to build a tower clock above his new stable at the manor house in Brocklesby Park.

Brocklesby tower beckoned Harrison, the church-steeple bell ringer, to a familiar high perch. Only this time, instead of swinging on a bell rope, he would mastermind a new instrument that would toil in its high turret, broadcasting the true time to all and sundry.

The tower clock that Harrison completed about 1722 still tells time in Brocklesby Park. It has been running continuously for more than 270 years—except for a brief period in 1884 when workers stopped it for refurbishing.

From its fine cabinet to its friction-free gearing, the clock reveals its maker as a master carpenter. For example, the works run without oil. The clock never needs lubrication, because the parts that would nor-

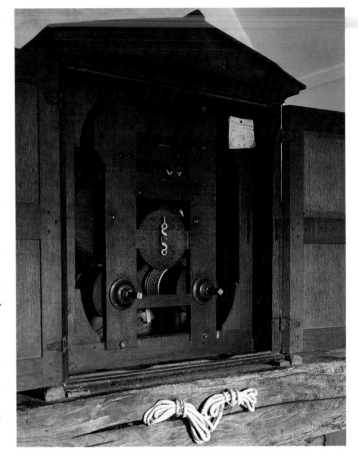

*The Brocklesby Park tower clock is housed in a finely made wooden cabinet in the loft above the stables. All the bearings are made of lignum vitae, a naturally oily hardwood that allows the clock to run without any lubricant. The escapement is the first version of Harrison's virtually friction-free escapement, the "grasshopper" escapement, so called because its action resembles the kicking of the hind legs of this insect.*

mally call for it were carved out of lignum vitae, a tropical hardwood that exudes its own grease. Harrison studiously avoided the use of iron or steel anywhere in the clockwork, for fear it would rust in the damp conditions. Wherever he needed metal, he installed parts made of brass.

When it came to fabricating toothed gears from oak, Harrison invented a new kind of wheel. Each of the wheels in the clock's going train resembles a child's drawing of the sun, with the lines of the wood grain radiating from the center of the wheel to the tips of the teeth as though drawn there with pencil and ruler. Harrison further guaranteed the wheel teeth their enduring structure by selecting the oak from fast-growing trees, whose growth rings formed widely spaced ripples in the trunks. Such trees yield lumber with a wide grain and great might, due to the high percentage of new wood.

*This illustration shows the areas of an oak tree from which Harrison carefully selected the wood suitable for the body and tooth segments of his wooden wheels. The body was taken from a plank running through the center of the trunk, in order to prevent the wheel from warping; the teeth were selected from the outside, where the more recent growth rings provided a suitably wider grain to give the teeth greater strength.*

(Under microscopic examination, growth rings resemble a honeycomb with hollows, while the new wood between the rings seems solid.) Elsewhere, wherever Harrison was willing to sacrifice strength for a lighter-weight material, as in the central portions of the wheels, he turned to slow-growing oak: With growth rings clinging closer together, this wood looks grainier and weighs less.

Harrison's intimate knowledge of wood is perhaps better appreciated in modern times, when hindsight and X-ray vision can validate the choices he made. Looking back, it's also obvious that Harrison took his first important step toward building a sea clock up there in the tower of Brocklesby Park — by eliminating the need for oil in the gears. A clock without oil, which till then was absolutely unheard of, would stand a much better chance of keeping time at sea than any clock yet built. For lubricants got thicker or thinner as temperatures dipped or soared over the course of a voyage, making the clock run faster or slower as a result — or cease running altogether.

As he built additional clocks, Harrison teamed up with his brother James, eleven years his junior but, like him, a superb craftsman. From 1725 to 1727 the brothers built two long-case, or grandfather, clocks. James Harrison signed them both in bold script right on their

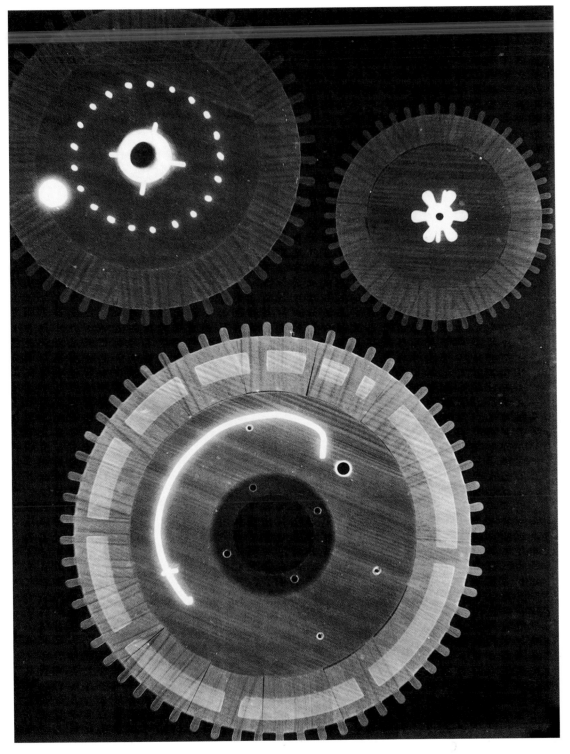

Harrison constructed his wheels so that the teeth had a radial grain to give them the required strength and overcome the possibility of breakage. This X-ray shows how the perfectly fitted radial grain segments were glued into a deep slot cut into the perimeter of the wheel. The wood was so well seasoned and carefully chosen that even after 250 years, the wheels are almost as good and true as they were when made.

*Harrison designed his "gridiron" pendulum to overcome the effect that a change in temperature would have on the length of a pendulum rod. With a rise in temperature, the downward expansion of the steel (blue) rods, which are suspended from the frames at the top, is counteracted by the upward expansion of the brass (yellow) rods, which are supported by the frames at the bottom. When the temperature falls, the upward contraction of the steel rods is counteracted by the downward contraction of the brass. Thus the pendulum's length (and hence its period of oscillation) remains constant. Fine adjustments to the compensation could be made with the "tin-whistle" adjuster, detailed in this illustration.*

painted wood faces. The name John Harrison does not appear anywhere, outside or inside, though there is not a horologist in the world who doubts that John was the designer and driving force in the construction of these clocks. Judging from recorded acts of John's generosity later in life, it appears that he gave his kid brother a boost by letting him put his own stamp on their joint venture.

Two fancy new gadgets enabled these grandfather clocks to keep nearly perfect time. These precision inventions of Harrison's came to be called the "gridiron" and the "grasshopper." You can see how the gridiron got its name if you peer through the small glass porthole on the case of the Harrison brothers' clock that stands against the back wall in Guildhall. The part of the pendulum that shows here consists of several alternating strips of two different metals, much like the parallel bars of the gridirons cooks used to broil meat. And this gridiron pendulum can truly stand the heat with no ill effects.

Most pendulums of Harrison's day expanded with heat, so they grew longer and ticked out time more slowly in hot weather. When cold made them contract, they speeded up the seconds, and threw the clock's rate off in the opposite direction. Every metal displayed this annoying tendency, though each metal stretched and shrank at its own characteristic rate. By combining long and short strips of two different metals—brass and steel—in one pendulum, Harrison eliminated the problem. The bound-together metals counteracted each other's changes in length as temperatures varied, so the pendulum never went too fast or too slow.

LEFT *This is the earliest of the three known longcase clocks produced by the Harrison brothers between 1725 and 1730 to test John Harrison's inventions for precision timekeeping. In outward appearance, they were designed to conform to the latest fashionable style so that they could be sold after the experiments had been conducted. While it appears that John was responsible for their design, all three were in fact signed and therefore made by his younger brother James.*

RIGHT *This particular clock, believed to have been made between 1725 and 1726, probably served as the test bed for many of Harrison's inventions. The upper wooden crosspiece of the movement frame has been charred by a candle flame. This may have occurred when someone, perhaps Harrison himself, was trying to get enough light into the movement to examine and adjust the grasshopper escapement.*

*As the pendulum swings to the right, the escapement pallet A comes into contact with a wheel tooth, which, via this pallet, then impulses the pendulum on its return to the left.*

*When pallet B is brought into contact with another tooth, the wheel recoils, releasing pallet A and allowing it to disengage from the wheel.*

*Through pallet B the pendulum is then impulsed to the right. These actions are controlled by the other component parts of the escapement.*

*An escapement provides the connection between the wheels of the timekeeper, which transmit the power and provide the indications of time, and the oscillator, which dictates the speed at which the clock runs. With each swing of the pendulum, the escapement has to allow one of the wheel teeth to escape and to transmit the power to maintain the pendulum's motion. Many ways have been devised to do this. The grasshopper escapement was designed to eliminate the friction and wear that affect stability in long-term performance.*

The grasshopper escapement—the part that counted the heartbeats of the clock's pacemaker—took its name from the motion of its crisscrossed components. These kicked like the hind legs of a leaping insect, quietly and without the friction that bedeviled existing escapement designs.

The Harrison brothers tested the accuracy of their gridiron-grasshopper clocks against the regular motions of the stars. The crosshairs of their homemade astronomical tracking instrument, with which they pinpointed the stars' positions, consisted of the border of a windowpane and the silhouette of the neighbor's chimney stack. Night after night, they marked the clock hour when given stars exited their field of view behind the chimney. From one night to the next, because of the Earth's rotation, a star should transit exactly 3 minutes, 56 seconds (of solar time) earlier than the previous night. Any clock that can track this sidereal schedule proves itself as perfect as God's magnificent clockwork.

In these late-night tests, the Harrisons' clocks never erred more than a single *second* in a whole *month*. In comparison, the very finest quality watches being produced any-

This view of the backplate of Harrison's precision longcase clock, c. 1725-26, shows the gridiron pendulum suspended from adjustable cycloidal cheeks. All of Harrison's innovations were designed to be finely adjusted as necessary when the clocks were undergoing tests. After conducting long trials under widely varying conditions, Harrison claimed that his clocks could keep time to within a second a month and would not need to be cleaned for forty or fifty years. These "regulators" provided the standard for testing the reliability and accuracy of his marine timekeepers.

*Taken about 1910, this photograph shows in the background a small lean-to addition adjacent to the front door of John Harrison's house. This was probably the "convenience" in which Harrison tested the coefficients of expansion of different metals. During the summer and winter of 1727-28, he conducted experiments there, with a contrivance mounted on the south-facing wall, to measure the expansion and contraction of brass, steel, and silver. The results enabled him to construct his gridiron pendulum, which maintained a constant length despite variations in temperature and thereby overcame one of the greatest problems of precision timekeeping.*

*John Harrison and his first wife purchased this seventeenth-century cottage in Barrow upon Humber on February 22, 1726. It was here that he tested the precision regulators and his first "sea clock," H-1. Despite efforts to save this historic structure, the cottage was demolished in November 1968 in order to build a second driveway to a seed merchant business. The site has now completely vanished under a new housing development constructed in 1994.*

where in the world at that time drifted off by about one *minute* every *day*. The only thing more remarkable than the Harrison clocks' extraordinary accuracy was the fact that such unprecedented precision had been achieved by a couple of country bumpkins working independently—and not by one of the masters such as Thomas Tompion or George Graham, who commanded expensive materials and experienced machinists in the clock centers of cosmopolitan London.

By the year 1727, Harrison recalled late in life, visions of the longitude prize had turned his mind to the special challenge of marine timekeeping. He realized he could make himself rich and famous by making his fine clocks seaworthy.

He'd already found a way around the problem of lubricants, hit a new high in precision with a virtually friction-free mechanism, and developed a pendulum for all seasons. He was ready to take on the salt air and the stormy sea. Ironically, Harrison saw he'd have to jettison his gridiron pendulum in order to win the £20,000.

Though the gridiron had triumphed on land, a pendulum was still a pendulum, and no pendulum could survive a rolling ocean. In place of the striated, swinging stick with its hanging bob, Harrison began picturing a springing set of seesaws, self-contained and counterbalanced to withstand the wildest waves.

When he had thought out the novel contraption to his own satisfaction, which took him almost four years, he set off for London—a journey of nearly two hundred miles—to lay his plan before the Board of Longitude.

*This equation of time table was prepared by Harrison and mounted inside a frame on the door of his 1728 regulator. In contrast to the equation table he made for his 1717 clock (p. 80), Harrison took into account the four-year cycle of the leap year when calculating this table.*

## CHAPTER EIGHT

# The Grasshopper Goes to Sea

Where in this small-talking world can I find
A longitude with no platitude?

CHRISTOPHER FRY, *The Lady's Not for Burning*

W HEN JOHN HARRISON ARRIVED in London in the summer of 1730, the Board of Longitude was nowhere to be found. Although that august body had been in existence for more than fifteen years, it occupied no official headquarters. In fact, it had never met.

So indifferent and mediocre were the proposals submitted to the board, that individual commissioners had simply sent out letters of rejection to the hopeful inventors. Not a single suggested solution had held enough promise to inspire any five commissioners—the minimum required by the Longitude Act for a quorum—to bother gathering together for a serious discussion of the method's merits.

Harrison, however, knew the identity of one of the most famous members of the Board of Longitude—the great Dr. Edmond Halley—and he headed straight for the Royal Observatory at Greenwich to find him.

Halley had become England's second astronomer royal in 1720, after John Flamsteed's death. The puritanical Flamsteed had reason to roll over in his grave at this development, since in life he had denounced Halley for drinking brandy and swearing

*John Harrison's first marine timekeeper, known as H-1, has four dials indicating seconds at the top, minutes on the left, hours on the right, and the day of the month at the bottom. This clock, which stands just over two feet tall and took five years to make, was completed in 1735.*

*When Harrison went to London to seek financial support for his proposed marine timekeeper, he probably took with him his twenty-two-page manuscript, the first and last pages of which are shown here. It summarizes his work to date, describing in detail his precision regulators and plans for a longitude timekeeper. On the final page, dated June 10, 1730, Harrison proposes to solve the longitude problem by locating one of his regulators at each port to serve as the standard for setting his "sea clocks."*

"like a sea-captain." And of course Flamsteed never forgave Halley, or his accomplice Newton, for pilfering the star catalogs and publishing them against his will.

Well liked by most, kind to his inferiors, Halley ran the observatory with a sense of humor. He added immeasurably to the luster of the place with his observations of the moon and his discovery of the proper motion of the stars—even if it's true what they say about the night he and Peter the Great cavorted like a couple of schoolboys and took turns pushing each other through hedges in a wheelbarrow.

Halley received Harrison politely. He listened intently to his concept for the sea clock. He was impressed with the drawings, and he said so. Yet Halley knew that the Board of Longitude would not welcome a mechanical answer to what it saw as an astronomical question. The board, it will be recalled, was top-heavy with astronomers, mathematicians, and navigators. Halley himself spent most of his days and nights working out the moon's motion to further the lunar distance method of finding longitude, yet he kept an open mind.

Rather than march Harrison into the lion's den, Halley sent him to see the well-known watchmaker George Graham. "Honest" George Graham, as he was later called, would be the best judge of the sea clock Harrison proposed to build. At least he would understand the fine points of its design.

Harrison feared Graham would steal the idea from him, but he followed Halley's advice anyway. What else could he do?

Graham, who was about twenty years older than Harrison, became his patron at the end of one long day together. As Harrison described their first meeting in his inimitable prose, "Mr Graham began as I thought very roughly with me, and the which had like to have occasioned me to become rough too; but however we got the ice broke . . . and indeed he became as at last vastly surprised at the thoughts or methods I had taken."

*George Graham (c. 1674-1751) was the most eminent maker of clocks and scientific instruments of his day. Born in a remote village in the north of England, he traveled to London when he was about fourteen and worked for the famous London clockmaker Thomas Tompion. He was elected a Fellow of the Royal Society in 1721 and later employed some of the leading makers of his time, including Thomas Mudge, John Bird, and John Shelton. John Harrison admitted that he owed a great deal to Graham's generous and unselfish support.*

Harrison went to see Graham at ten o'clock in the morning, and by eight that evening they were still talking shop. Graham, the premier scientific instrument maker and a Fellow of the Royal Society, invited Harrison, the village carpenter, to stay to dinner. When Graham finally said good night, he waved Harrison back to Barrow with every encouragement, including a generous loan, to be repaid with no great haste and at no interest.

Harrison spent the next five years piecing together the first sea clock, which has come to be called Harrison's No. 1, for it marked the first in a series of attempts — H-1 for short. His brother James helped, though neither one of them signed the timepiece, strangely enough. The going train ran on wooden wheels, as in the pair's previous collaborations. But overall, it looked like no other clock ever seen before or since.

Built of brightly shining brass, with rods and balances sticking out at odd angles, its broad bottom and tall projections recall some ancient vessel that never existed. It looks like a cross between a galley and a galleon, with a high, ornate stern facing forward, two towering masts that carry no sails, and knobbed brass oars to be manned by tiers of unseen rowers. It is a model ship, escaped from its bottle, afloat on the sea of time.

The numbered dials on H-1's face obviously tie it to the telling of time: One dial marks the hours, another counts the minutes, a third ticks off the seconds, and the last denotes the days of the month. Yet the look of the whole contrivance, fairly bristling with complexity, suggests that it must be something more than just a perfect time-keeper. The large coiled springs and unfamiliar machinery tempt one to try to commandeer the thing and ride it into another era. No fanciful movie about time travel, despite the best efforts of Hollywood set design, ever presented a time machine as convincing as this one.

The Harrisons housed H-1, which weighs seventy-five pounds, in a glazed cabinet four feet in every dimension—high, wide, and deep. The case may have hidden the whirligig aspects of the timepiece. Perhaps only the face, with its four dials surrounded by eight carved cherubs and four crowns in a tangle of serpentine ropes or leafless vines, showed from the outside. However, the cabinet, like the cases of Harrison's early clocks, has been lost, exposing the works to general scrutiny. H-1 now lives and works (with daily winding) in an armored-glass box at the National Maritime Museum in Greenwich, where it still runs gamely in all its friction-free glory, much to the delight of visitors. The decorated face clashes with the skeletal works—the way a well-dressed woman might look if she stood behind an imaging screen that bared her beating heart.

Even at the start of its long career, H-1 constituted a study in contrasts. It was of its age but ahead of its time, and when it came along, the world was already weary of waiting for it. Although H-1 did what it set out to do, it performed so singularly that people were perplexed by its success.

The gridirons, positioned in the center of H-1 toward the back, compensate for variations in temperature by adjusting the effective length of the helical balance springs that control the period of oscillation of the bar balances. The balances, which have polished brass balls of equal weight on each end, are linked in a virtually friction-free manner at the center with two flat brass ribbons so that the motion of the ship will not affect their oscillation.

The Harrison brothers took H-1 out for trial runs on a barge on the River Humber. Then John carried it to London in 1735, and delivered on his promise to George Graham.

Much pleased, Graham showed the wonderful sea clock—not to the Board of Longitude but to the Royal Society, who gave it a hero's welcome. Concurring with Dr. Halley and three other equally impressed Fellows of the Society, Graham wrote this endorsement of H-1 and its maker:

> John Harrison, having with great labour and expense, contrived and executed a Machine for measuring time at sea, upon such Principle, as seem to us to Promise a very great and sufficient degree of Exactness. We are of Opinion, it highly deserves Public Encouragement, In order to a thorough Tryal and Improvement, of the severall Contrivances, for preventing those Irregularityes in time, that naturally arise from the different degrees of Heat and Cold, a moist and drye Temperature of the Air, and the Various Agitations of the ship.

Despite the hoopla, the Admiralty dragged its feet for a year in arranging the trial. Then, instead of sending H-1 to the West Indies, as the Longitude Act required, the admirals ordered Harrison to take his clock down to Spithead and board H.M.S. *Centurion*, bound for Lisbon. The First Lord of the Admiralty, Sir Charles Wager, sent the following letter of introduction to Captain Proctor, commander of the *Centurion*, on May 14, 1736:

> Sir, The Instrument which is put on Board your Ship, has been approved by all the Mathematicians in Town that have seen it, (and few have not) to be the Best that has been made for measuring Time; how it will succeed at Sea, you will be a Judge; I have writ to Sir John Norris, to desire him to send home the Instrument and the Maker of it (who I think you have with you) by the first Ship that comes . . . [T]he Man is said by those who know him best, to be a very ingenious and sober Man, and capable of finding out something more than he has already, if he can find Encouragement; I desire therefore, that you will let the Man be used civilly, and that you will be as kind to him as you can.

Captain Proctor wrote back right away to say,

> [T]he Instrument is placed in my Cabbin, for giving the Man all the
> Advantage that is possible for making his Observations, and I find him to be a
> very sober, a very industrious, and withal a very modest Man, so that my good
> Wishes can't but attend him; but the Difficulty of measuring Time truly, where
> so many unequal Shocks, and Motions, stand in Opposition to it, gives me
> concern for the honest Man, and makes me fear he has attempted
> Impossibilities; but Sir, I will do him all the Good, and give him all the Help,
> that is in my Power, and acquaint him with your Concern for his Success, and
> your Care that he shall be well treated . . .

Proctor needn't have worried about the performance of Harrison's machine. It was the man's stomach that gave him grief. The rough crossing kept the clockmaker hanging over the rail much of the time, when he wasn't in the captain's cabin, tending his timekeeper. What a pity Harrison couldn't fit his own insides with the two dumbbell-shaped bar balances and four helical balance springs that helped H-1 keep its equanimity throughout the journey. Mercifully, the strong winds blew the *Centurion* swiftly to Lisbon within one week.

The good Captain Proctor died suddenly as soon as the ship reached harbor, before he'd written up any account of the voyage in his log. Only four days later, Roger Wills, master of H.M.S. *Orford*, received instructions to sail Harrison back to England. The weather, which Wills recorded as "very mixed with gales and calms," made for a monthlong voyage home.

When the ship neared land at last, Wills assumed it to be the Start, a well-known point on the south coast around Dartmouth. That was where his reckoning placed the ship. Harrison, however, going by his sea clock, countered that the land sighted must be the Lizard on the Penzance peninsula, more than sixty miles west of the Start. And so it was.

H-1 was sent on a trial to Lisbon in 1736. On the return voyage, after four weeks of gales and calms, land was sighted in the distance. The sailors believed it to be Start Point, but Harrison, observing the time shown on his clock, claimed that it was the Lizard. As they came closer, the sailors realized that Harrison was right. His clock had corrected the longitude of the ship by sixty-eight miles.

This correction greatly impressed Master Wills. Later, he swore out an affidavit admitting his own mistake and praising the accuracy of the timekeeper. Wills gave this certificate, dated June 24, 1737, to Harrison as an official pat on the back. It marked the start of a banner week for Harrison, because on the 30th, the commissioners of the Board of Longitude convened for the very first time—twenty-three years after the board was created—citing his marvelous machine as the occasion.

Harrison presented himself and H-1 to the eight commissioners who sat in judgment of his work. He recognized several friendly faces among them. In addition to Dr. Halley, already a booster, he saw Sir Charles of the Admiralty, who had written the letter of concern on the eve of H-1's maiden voyage, urging that Harrison get a fair shake. And there was Admiral Norris, head of the fleet at Lisbon, who had given Harrison his sailing orders. The two academics in attendance, Dr. Robert Smith, the Plumian Professor of Astronomy at Cambridge, and Dr. James Bradley, the Savilian Professor of Astronomy at Oxford, also supported Harrison, as both of them had signed their names to the letter of endorsement that Graham wrote on behalf of the

Royal Society. Dr. Smith even shared Harrison's interest in music and had his own odd views on the musical scale. Sir Hans Sloane, president of the Royal Society, rounded out the scientific representation at the meeting. The other two board members, unknown to Harrison, were the Right Honorable Arthur Onslow, speaker of the House of Commons, and Lord Monson, commissioner of Lands and Plantations, who reflected the board's political clout.

Harrison had everything to gain. He stood there with his prized possession, before a group of professionals and politicians predisposed to be proud of what he'd done for king and country. He had every right to demand a West Indies trial, to prove H-1 deserving of the £20,000 promised in the Longitude Act. But he was too much of a perfectionist to do it.

Instead, Harrison pointed out the foibles of H-1. He was the only person in the room to say anything at all critical of the sea clock, which had not erred more than a few seconds in twenty-four hours to or from Lisbon on the trial run. Still, Harrison said it showed some "defects" that he wanted to correct. He conceded he needed to do a bit more tinkering with the mechanism. He could also make the clock a lot smaller, he thought. With another two years' work, if the board could see its way clear to advancing him some funds for further development, he could produce another timekeeper. An even better timekeeper. And then he would come back to the board and request an official trial on a voyage to the West Indies. But not now.

The board gave its stamp of approval to an offer it couldn't refuse. As for the £500 Harrison wanted as seed money, the board promised to pay half of it as soon as possible. Harrison could claim the other half once he had turned over the finished product to a ship's captain of the Royal Navy, ready for a road test. At that point, according to the agreement recorded in the minutes of the meeting, Harrison would either accompany the new timekeeper to the West Indies himself, or appoint "some proper Person" to go in his stead. (Perhaps the commissioners had heard tell of Harrison's seasickness and were already making allowances for him.)

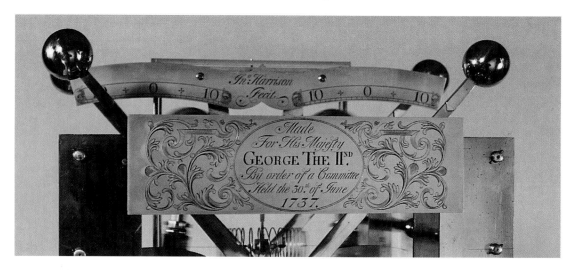

One last provision completed the compact. Upon the return of the second time-keeper from its trial at sea, Harrison would surrender it, along with the first sea clock, "for the Use of the Public."

A better businessman might have balked at this point. Indeed, Harrison could have argued that while the board was entitled to the second machine, as thanks for its sub-sidy, it had no claim to the first, which he had built at his own expense. But, rather than quibble over rights of ownership, he took the board's proprietary interest as a positive incentive. He inferred that he was in their employ now, like an artist commis-sioned to create a great work for the throne, and so would be royally rewarded.

Harrison wrote this assumption prominently, a bit pompously, on the face of the sec-ond timekeeper when he finished it. Above the austere, unornamented dial of H-2 is an engraved silvered plate, with flourishes of scrolls surrounding the inscription, "Made for His Majesty George The IInd, By order of a Committee Held on 30th of June 1737."

If Harrison harbored any illusions of grandeur about H-2, he dashed them himself in short order. By the time he presented the new clock to the Board of Longitude in January 1741, he was already disgusted with it. He gave the commissioners something of a repeat performance of his previous appearance before them: All he really wanted, he said, was their blessing to go home and try again. As a result, H-2 never went to sea.

*H-2 is taller but occupies considerably less space than its predecessor, H-1, which with case and gimbals must have taken up a large area of the captain's cabin. Although completed in only two years, H-2 was never tried at sea, because Harrison discovered during tests that it had some inherent faults that could not easily be remedied. Therefore he abandoned it and began to construct his third machine.*

*This side view of H-2 shows the remontoire, a device that Harrison designed to provide a more constant source of power to the escapement. H-2 is essentially a refined version of H-1, with all the wheels made of brass and various other details that would improve its performance and reliability on an ocean voyage.*

The second timekeeper, which had turned out to be a brass heavyweight of eighty-six pounds (although it did fit into a smaller box, as promised), was every inch as extraordinary as the first. It embodied several new improvements—including a mechanism to ensure a uniform drive and a more responsive temperature compensation device, each of which constituted a minor revolution in precision. Also the whole machine passed many rigorous tests with flying colors. The 1741-42 report of the Royal Society says that these tests subjected H-2 to heating, to cooling, and to being "agitated for many hours together, with greater violence than what it could receive from the motion of a ship in a storm."

Not only did H-2 survive this drubbing but it won full backing from the Society: "And the Result of these Experiments, is this; that (as far as can be determined without making a voyage to sea) the motion is sufficiently regular and exact, for finding the Longitude of a Ship within the nearest Limits proposed by Parliament and probably much nearer."

But it wasn't good enough for Harrison. The same viselike conviction that led him to his finest innovations—along his own lines of thinking, without regard for the opinions of others—rendered him deaf to praise. What did it matter what the Royal Society thought of H-2, if its mechanism did not pass muster with him?

Harrison, now a London resident and forty-eight years old, faded into his workshop and was hardly heard from during the nearly twenty years he devoted to the completion of H-3, which he called his "curious third machine." He emerged only to request and collect from the board occasional stipends of £500, as he slogged through the difficulties of transforming the bar-shaped balances of the first two timekeepers into the circular balance wheels that graced the third.

Meanwhile, H-1 stayed in the limelight. Graham had it on loan from Harrison, and kept it on exhibit in his shop, where people came from all over just to look at it.

Pierre Le Roy of Paris, the deserving heir to his father Julien Le Roy's title of king's clockmaker in France, paid tribute to H-1. Upon his 1738 visit to London, he called the timekeeper "a most ingenious contrivance." Le Roy's archrival, the Swiss-born horologist Ferdinand Berthoud, echoed that sentiment when he first saw H-1 in 1763.

The English artist William Hogarth, well known for his obsession with time and timekeeping, who had actually started out as an engraver of watchcases, took a particular interest in H-1. Hogarth had portrayed a "longitude lunatic," scribbling a dimwitted solution to the longitude problem on the walls of Bedlam Asylum, in his popular work *The Rake's Progress* of 1735. Now, H-1 had elevated the whole subject of finding longitude from the status of a joke to the highest level of combined art and science. Writing in his *Analysis of Beauty*, published in 1753, Hogarth described H-1 as "one of the most exquisite movements ever made."

ABOVE *While testing H-2, Harrison discovered that if the timekeeper was subjected to a sudden forward-backward motion, the period of oscillation of its bar balances could be affected by centrifugal force. The mechanism he designed to overcome this problem is shown in this drawing: H-3 incorporates two large and heavy seconds-beating balances, mounted one above the other and linked by thin brass ribbons.*

LEFT *Delineating how deeply "the longitude problem" permeated society, the English artist William Hogarth in 1735 depicted a "longitude lunatic" in the last of his famous series of eight prints entitled* The Rake's Progress.

## CHAPTER NINE

# Hands on Heaven's Clock

The moving Moon went up the sky,
And no where did abide:
Softly she was going up,
And a star or two beside,

SAMUEL TAYLOR COLERIDGE, "The Rime of the Ancient Mariner"

T HE MOVING MOON, full, gibbous, or crescent-shaped, shone at last for the navigators of the eighteenth century like a luminous hand on the clock of heaven. The broad expanse of sky served as dial for this celestial clock, while the sun, the planets, and the stars painted the numbers on its face.

A seaman could not read the clock of heaven with a quick glance but only with complex observing instruments, with combinations of sightings taken together and repeated as many as seven times in a row for accuracy's sake, and with logarithm tables compiled far in advance by human computers for the convenience of sailors on long voyages. It took about four hours to calculate the time from the heavenly dial — when the weather was clear, that is. If clouds appeared, the clock hid behind them.

The clock of heaven formed John Harrison's chief competition for the longitude prize; the lunar distance method for finding longitude, based on measuring the motions of the moon, constituted the only reasonable alternative to Harrison's time-keepers. By a grand confluence, Harrison produced his sea clocks at precisely the

*John Hadley (1682-1744), an optical instrument maker who considerably improved the grinding and polishing of lenses, was elected a Fellow of the Royal Society in 1717 and appointed its vice president in 1728. At the Royal Society on May 13, 1731, he described two reflecting quadrants he had invented. The first was an instrument for improving the accuracy of lunar distance measurements, and the second was intended more specifically for measuring the altitude of the sun, the moon, or a star above the horizon at sea. The latter device represented a major advance in navigational instrumentation and became known as Hadley's quadrant.*

*Hadley's quadrant allowed the mariner to measure the altitude of the sun or a star by aligning its reflected image with the plane of the horizon. Since it was easier to use and had greater accuracy than its predecessors (the cross-staff and the backstaff), this instrument was quickly adopted by mariners for finding latitude at sea and continued to be employed throughout the nineteenth century.*

same period when scientists finally amassed the theories, instruments, and information needed to make use of the clock of heaven.

In longitude determination, a realm of endeavor where nothing had worked for centuries, suddenly two rival approaches of apparently equal merit ran neck and neck. Perfection of the two methods blazed parallel trails of development down the decades from the 1730s to the 1760s. Harrison, ever the loner, pursued his own quiet course through a maze of clockwork machinery, while his opponents, the professors of astronomy and mathematics, promised the moon to merchants, mariners, and Parliament.

In 1731, the year after Harrison wrote out the recipe for H-1 in words and pictures, two inventors—one English, one American—independently created the long-sought instrument upon which the lunar distance method depended. Annals of the history of science give equal credit to John Hadley, the country squire who first demonstrated this instrument to the Royal Society, and Thomas Godfrey, the indigent Philadelphia glazier who was struck, almost simultaneously, by the same inspiration. (Later it was discovered that Sir Isaac Newton had *also* drawn plans for a nearly identical device, but the description got lost until long after Newton's death in a mountain of paperwork left with Edmond Halley. Halley himself, as well as Robert Hooke before him, had sketched out similar designs for the same purpose.)

Most British sailors called the instrument Hadley's (not Godfrey's) quadrant, quite understandably. Some dubbed it an octant, because its curved scale formed the eighth part of a circle; others preferred the name reflecting quadrant, pointing out that the machine's mirrors doubled its capacity. By any name, the instrument soon helped sailors find their latitude *and* longitude.

Older instruments, from the astrolabe to the cross-staff to the backstaff, had been used for centuries to determine latitude and local time by gauging the height of the sun or a given star above the horizon. But now, thanks to a trick done with paired mirrors, the new reflecting quadrant allowed direct measurement of the elevations of two celestial bodies, as well as the distances between them. Even if the ship pitched and rolled, the objects in the navigator's sights retained their relative positions vis-à-vis one another. The quadrant quickly evolved into an even more accurate device, called a sextant, which incorporated a telescope and a wider measuring arc. These additions permitted the precise determination of the ever-changing, telltale distances between the moon and the sun during daylight hours, or between the moon and stars after dark.

With detailed star charts and a trusty instrument, a good navigator could now stand on the deck of his ship and measure the lunar distances. (Actually, many of the more careful navigators sat, the better to steady themselves, and the real sticklers lay down flat on their backs.) Next he consulted a table that listed the angular distances between the moon and numerous celestial objects for various hours of the day, as they would be observed from London or Paris. (As their name implies, angular distances are expressed in degrees of arc; they describe the size of the angle created by two lines of sight, running from the observer's eye to the pair of objects in question.) He then compared the time when he saw the moon thirty degrees away from the star Regulus, say, in the heart of Leo the Lion, with the time that particular position had been predicted for the home port. If, for example, this navigator's observation occurred at one o'clock in the morning, local time, when the tables called for the same configuration over London at 4 A.M., then the ship's time was three hours earlier—and the ship itself, therefore, at longitude forty-five degrees west of London.

"I say, Old Boy, do you smoke?" a brazen sun asked of the moon in an old English log book cartoon portraying the lunar distance method. "No, you brute," the skittish moon replied. "Keep your distance!"

Hadley's quadrant capitalized on the work of astronomers, who had cemented the positions of the fixed stars on the celestial clock dial. John Flamsteed alone personally donated some forty man-years to the monumental effort of mapping the heavens. As the first astronomer royal, Flamsteed conducted 30,000 individual observations, all dutifully recorded and confirmed with telescopes he built himself or bought at his own expense. Flamsteed's finished star catalog tripled the number of entries in the sky atlas Tycho Brahe had compiled at Uranienborg in Denmark, and improved the precision of the census by several orders of magnitude.

Limited as he was to the skies over Greenwich, Flamsteed was glad to see the flamboyant Edmond Halley take off for the South Atlantic in 1676, right after the founding of the Royal Observatory. Halley set up a mini-Greenwich on the island of St. Helena. It was the right place but the wrong atmosphere, and Halley counted only 341 new stars through the haze. Nevertheless, this achievement earned him a flattering reputation as "the southern Tycho."

During his own tenure as astronomer royal, from 1720 to 1742, Halley studiously tracked the moon. The mapping of the heavens, after all, was merely a prelude to the more challenging problem of charting the moon's course through the fields of stars.

The moon follows an irregular elliptical orbit around the Earth, so that the moon's distance from the Earth and relation to the background stars is in constant flux. What's more, since the moon's orbital motion varies cyclically over an eighteen-year period, eighteen years' worth of data constitute the bare minimum groundwork for any meaningful predictions of the moon's position.

Halley not only observed the moon day and night, to reveal the intricacies of her motions, he also pored through ancient eclipse records for clues about her past. Any and all data regarding lunar orbital motions might be grist for creating the tables navi-

*This thirteen-inch-radius Hadley's quadrant, dated 1750, is inscribed with the owner's name, Captain Alexander Caldwell. In order to reduce weight, most of these instruments had frames made of wood; in this example, brass has been used for the degree plate, which is engraved with a diagonal scale, and for the index arm, which has divisions for reading an observation to three minutes of a degree. Because of the reflecting principles of this instrument, the ninety-degree scale of a Hadley's quadrant is contained in an arc of forty-five degrees. Since the frame thereby occupies one-eighth of a circle, this instrument later became known as an octant, in order to distinguish it from the similar, but larger and more sophisticated, sextant.*

gators needed. Halley concluded from these sources that the moon's rate of revolution about the Earth was accelerating over time. (Today, scientists assert that the moon is not speeding up; rather, the Earth's rotation is slowing down, braked by tidal friction, but Halley was correct in noting a relative change.)

Even before he became astronomer royal, Halley had made predictions regarding the return of the comet that immortalized his name. He also showed, in 1718, that three of the brightest stars had changed their positions in the heavens over the two millennia since Greek and Chinese astronomers had plotted their whereabouts. Just within the century-plus since Tycho's maps, Halley found that these three stars had shifted slightly. Nevertheless, Halley assured sailors that this "proper motion" of the stars, though it stands as one of his greatest discoveries, was only barely perceptible over eons, and would not mar the utility of the clock of heaven.

*James Bradley (1693-1762) began his career in the church, but his interest in astronomy brought him to the notice of Edmond Halley, through whose influence he was elected a Fellow of the Royal Society in 1718, when he was twenty-five. Through his subsequent appointment as Savilian Professor of Astronomy at Oxford in 1721, he became an ex officio member of the Board of Longitude. This portrait was painted after he succeeded Halley as astronomer royal in 1742. Bradley was one of John Harrison's early supporters, along with Halley and other Fellows of the Royal Society.*

At the age of eighty-three, while he was still hale and hearty, Halley tried to pass the torch as astronomer royal to his heir apparent, James Bradley, but the king (George II) wouldn't hear of it. Bradley had to wait to take office until after Halley died, nearly two years later, just a couple of weeks past Christmas Day in January 1742. The inauguration of the new astronomer royal presaged a drastic reversal of fortune for John Harrison, whom Halley had always admired. Bradley, despite his 1735 endorsement of the sea clock, felt little affinity for anything outside astronomy.

Bradley had distinguished himself early in his career by trying to gauge the distance to the stars. Although he failed to find the actual size of this gap, his efforts with a telescope twenty-four feet long provided the first hard evidence that the Earth really did move through space. As a result of this same failed attempt to measure stellar distances, Bradley arrived at a new, *true* value for the speed of light, improving on Ole Roemer's earlier estimate. He also determined the shockingly large diameter of Jupiter, and detected tiny deviations in the tilt of the Earth's axis, which he correctly blamed on the pull of the moon.

Once ensconced at Greenwich, Astronomer Royal Bradley, like Flamsteed and Halley before him, took the perfection of navigation as his primary mission. He out-Flamsteeded Flamsteed with his precision maps of the heavens—and his modest refusal of a raise in pay when it was offered to him.

The Paris Observatory, meanwhile, redoubled the efforts at Greenwich. Picking up where Halley had left off years earlier, French astronomer Nicolas Louis de Lacaille headed for the Cape of Good Hope in 1750. There he cataloged nearly two thousand southern stars over Africa. Lacaille left his brand on the skies of the nether hemisphere by defining several new constellations, and naming them after the great beasts of his own contemporary pantheon—Telescopium, Microscopium, Sextans (the Sextant), and Horologium (the Clock).

In this fashion, astronomers built one of the three pillars supporting the lunar distance method: They established the positions of the stars and studied the motion of the moon. Inventors had put up another pillar by giving sailors the means to measure the critical distances between the moon and the sun or other stars. All that remained for the refinement of the method were the detailed lunar tables that could translate the instrument readings into longitude positions. The creation of these lunar ephemerides

*Nicolas Louis de Lacaille (1713-62), one of the leading French astronomers of the eighteenth century, made observations of the southern skies during an expedition to the Cape of Good Hope between 1750 and 1752. He gave some of the new constellations he observed the names of popular scientific instruments.*

Tobias Mayer (1723-62) made the breakthrough that enabled the lunar distance method to become a practicable way of finding longitude at sea. As a young man, he displayed an interest in cartography and mathematics. In 1750, he was appointed professor in the Georg-August Academy in Göttingen, where he was able to devote more time to his interests in lunar theory and the longitude problem. From 1751 to 1755, he had an extensive correspondence with Leonhard Euler, whose work on differential equations enabled Mayer to calculate lunar distance tables.

turned out to be the hardest part of the problem. The complexities of the moon's orbit thwarted progress in predicting lunar-solar and lunar-stellar distances.

Thus Bradley received with great interest the set of lunar tables compiled by a German mapmaker, Tobias Mayer, who claimed to have provided this missing link. Mayer thought he could lay claim to the longitude prize, too, which inspired him to send his idea, along with a new circular observing instrument, to Lord Anson of the English Admiralty, a member of the Board of Longitude. (This same George Anson, now first lord of the Admiralty, had commanded the *Centurion* on her dismal tour of the South Pacific between Cape Horn and Juan Fernández Island in 1741.) Admiral Lord Anson turned the tables over to Bradley for evaluation.

Mayer, the mapmaker, worked in Göttingen, nailing down precise coordinates for the productions of the Homann Cartographic Bureau. He used, among his many tools, the eclipses of the moon and lunar occultations of the stars (that is, the predicted disappearance of certain stars as the moon moved in front of them). Although he focused on land maps, Mayer had to rely on the moon for fixing positions in time and space, just as a sailor would. And in the course of meeting his own needs for predicting the lunar positions, he grasped an advance that applied directly to the longitude problem; he created the first set of lunar tables for the moon's location at twelve-hour intervals. He drew invaluable help in this enterprise from his four-year correspondence with the Swiss mathematician Leonhard Euler, who had reduced the relative movements of the sun, the Earth, and the moon to a series of elegant equations.

Bradley compared Mayer's projections with hundreds of observations he took himself at Greenwich. The match excited him, because Mayer never missed an angular distance by more than 1.5 minutes of arc. This accuracy could mean finding longitude to within half a degree—and that was the magic number for the top prize stated in the Longitude Act. In 1757, the same year the manuscript tables came into his hands, Bradley arranged to have them tested at sea by Captain John Campbell aboard the *Essex*. The testing continued on subsequent voyages off the coast of Brittany, despite

*Leonhard Euler (1707-83) was one of the most outstanding mathematicians of the eighteenth century. At age twenty, he was invited to the St. Petersburg Academy and six years later succeeded Daniel Bernoulli as professor of mathematics there. Euler's pioneering work on differential equations enabled Tobias Mayer to make lunar distances a viable method of finding longitude at sea. In recognition of his contribution, the Board of Longitude awarded Euler £300 in 1765.*

LEFT *In an undated letter to the Board of Longitude, Mayer requested a reward for his lunar distance tables and the accompanying instructions for using them to find longitude at sea. Mayer did not live long enough to see his prize. The Board of Longitude granted £3,000 to his heirs in 1765, after his tables had been used successfully during the second trial of H-4.*

RIGHT *Tobias Mayer's* Tabulae Motuum Solis et Lunae Novae et Correctae [New and Correct Tables of the Motions of the Sun and Moon] *is an edited version of the manuscript that his widow presented to the Board of Longitude in 1763. Under the direction of Nevil Maskelyne, 2,000 copies were printed in 1770.*

the Seven Years War, and the lunar distance method swelled with new promise. After the thirty-nine-year-old Mayer died of an infection in 1762, the board awarded his widow £3,000 in recognition of the work he had done. Another £300 went to Euler, for his founding theorems.

Thus the lunar distance method was propagated by individual investigators scattered all across the globe, each one doing his small part on a project of immense proportions. No wonder the technique assumed an air of planet-wide importance.

Even the difficulty of taking lunar distances, or lunars, as they came to be called, augmented their respectability. In addition to the need for measuring the altitudes of the various heavenly bodies and the angular distances between them, a navigator had to factor in the objects' nearness to the horizon, where the steep refraction of light would put their apparent positions considerably above their actual positions. The navigator also battled the problem of lunar parallax, since the tables were formulated for an observer at the center of the Earth, while a ship rides the waves at about sea level, and the sailor on the quarterdeck might stand a good twenty feet higher than that. Such factors required rectifying by the appropriate calculations. Clearly, a man who mastered the mathematical manipulation of all this arcane information, while still keeping his sea legs, could justly congratulate himself.

The admirals and astronomers on the Board of Longitude openly endorsed the heroic lunar distance method, even in its formative stages, as the logical outgrowth of

*To find longitude by the lunar distance method, a mariner had to make three almost simultaneous angular measurements and determine the time of their observation. These were the altitude of the moon above the horizon, the altitude of the star (or sun) above the horizon, and the distance of the moon from the star (or the sun). After making the necessary calculations to find the center distances and adjusting for the effects of refraction, parallax, and dip of the horizon, the navigator consulted lunar distance tables to determine the time this observation occurred at the reference point for which the tables were calculated. The difference between the local time of the ship and the time shown in the tables could then be used to calculate the longitude of the ship.*

117

their own life experience with sea and sky. By the late 1750s the technique finally looked practicable, thanks to the cumulative efforts of the many contributors to this large-scale international enterprise.

In comparison, John Harrison offered the world a little ticking thing in a box. Preposterous!

Worse, this device of Harrison's had all the complexity of the longitude problem already hardwired into its works. The user didn't have to master math or astronomy or gain experience to make it go. Something unseemly attended the sea clock, in the eyes of scientists and celestial navigators. Something facile. Something flukish. In an earlier era, Harrison might have been accused of witchcraft for proposing such a magic-box solution. As it was, Harrison stood alone against the vested navigational interests of the scientific establishment. He became entrenched in this position by virtue of his own high standards and the high degree of skepticism expressed by his opponents. Instead of the accolades he might have expected for his achievements, he was to be subjected to many unpleasant trials that began after the completion of his masterpiece, the fourth timekeeper, H-4, in 1759.

*This sextant of fifteen-inch radius, made by Jesse Ramsden, London, c. 1772, is one of the Board of Longitude instruments reputed to have been used aboard the* Discovery *on Captain Cook's third voyage. The sextant, so called because its frame describes one-sixth of a circle, was developed from the octant specifically for the purpose of making lunar distance measurements. Made entirely of brass, it was fitted with a telescope and accommodated on its 120-degree scale a vernier, allowing readings accurate to one minute of arc.*

## CHAPTER TEN

# The Diamond Timekeeper

The cabinet is formed of gold
And pearl and crystal shining bright,
And within it opens into a world
And a little lovely moony night.

WILLIAM BLAKE, "The Crystal Cabinet"

ROME WASN'T BUILT IN A DAY, they say. Even a small part of Rome, the Sistine Chapel, took eight years to construct, plus another eleven years to decorate, with Michelangelo sprawled atop his scaffolding from 1508 to 1512, frescoing scenes from the Old Testament on the ceiling. Fourteen years passed from the conception to the casting of the Statue of Liberty. The carving of the Mount Rushmore Monument likewise spanned a period of fourteen years. The Suez and Panama Canals each took about ten years to excavate, and it was arguably ten years from the decision to put a man on the moon to the successful landing of the *Apollo* lunar module.

It took John Harrison nineteen years to build H-3.

Historians and biographers cannot explain why Harrison—who turned out a turret clock in two years flat when he had scant experience to guide him, and who made two revolutionary sea clocks within nine years—should have lingered so long in the workshop with H-3. No one suggests that the workaholic Harrison dallied or became distracted. Indeed, there is evidence that he did nothing *but* work on H-3, almost to the detriment of his health and family, since the project kept him from pursuing most

*At the second meeting of the Board of Longitude, in 1741, Harrison announced that he was constructing a third timekeeper, which he expected to have ready for trial in two years. H-3 was, however, to present its maker with several almost insurmountable difficulties and was not ready for trial until 1760, about nineteen years after it was started. But by this time Harrison had begun creating a much smaller timekeeper, and H-3, like its predecessor, was never tried at sea. This timekeeper was even smaller than H-2, standing only 23.2 inches in overall height.*

other gainful employment. Although he took on a few mundane clockmaking jobs to make ends meet, his recorded income during this period seems to have come entirely from the Board of Longitude, which granted him several extensions on his deadline and five payments of £500 each.

*The Copley Medal, the Royal Society's highest distinction, was struck with these dies and then engraved with the name of the recipient and the date. This gold medal, usually awarded annually, was given to John Harrison in 1749 for the improvements he had achieved in precision timekeeping. At that time, Harrison had been working on his third marine timekeeper for almost nine years, but no end was yet in sight.*

The Royal Society, which had been founded in the previous century as a prestigious scientific discussion group, rallied behind Harrison all through these trying years. His friend George Graham and other admiring members of the society insisted that Harrison leave his workbench long enough to accept the Copley Gold Medal on November 30, 1749. (Later recipients of the Copley Medal include Benjamin Franklin, Henry Cavendish, Joseph Priestley, Captain James Cook, Ernest Rutherford, and Albert Einstein.)

Harrison's Royal Society supporters eventually followed the medal, which was the highest tribute they could confer, with an offer of Fellowship in the Society. This would have put the prestigious initials F.R.S. after his name. But Harrison declined. He asked that the membership be given to his son William instead. As Harrison must have known, Fellowship in the Royal Society is *earned* by scientific achievement; it cannot ordinarily be transferred, even to one's next of kin, in the manner of a property deed. Nevertheless, William was duly elected to membership in his own right in 1765.

This sole surviving son of John Harrison took up his father's cause. Though a child when the work on the sea clocks began, William passed through his teens and twenties in the company of H-3. He continued working faithfully with his father on the longitude timekeepers until he was forty-five years old, shepherding them through their trials and supporting the elder Harrison through his tribulations with the Board of Longitude.

As for the challenge of H-3, which contains 753 separate parts, the Harrisons seem to have taken it in their stride. They never cursed the instrument or rued its long rule over their lives. In a retrospective review of his career milestones, John Harrison wrote of H-3 with gratitude for the hard lessons it taught him: "[H]ad it not been through some transactions I had with my third machine . . . and as to be so very weighty or so highly useful a matter or discovery and as never to be known or discovered without it . . . and worth all the money and time it cost viz my curious third machine."

*This unsigned and undated oil painting is reputed to be a self-portrait by William Harrison (1728-1815), who lived the life of an affluent gentleman after inheriting most of the remaining prize money and many of his father's possessions. There is good evidence, however, to suggest that the young man in the portrait is in fact William's son, John (1761-1842).*

# DETAILS OF H-3

Harrison prepared these instructions to aid in the assembly of H-3. Lieutenant Commander Rupert T. Gould, who spent seven years in the late 1920s and early 1930s restoring this machine, commented on the extraordinarily complex and time-consuming task of assembling and disassembling the mechanism, which he had to repeat many times to make various adjustments. This list illustrates the procedures that had to be followed and shows one of the reasons why H-3 took Harrison so long to perfect.

This illustration of H-3 is one of a series of drawings made in about 1840, when it was undergoing restoration. The disk screwed to the plate in the lower right corner is the cover of the first caged roller bearing, invented by Harrison to reduce friction. This device is the forerunner of the caged ball bearing, which is so widely used in engineering today.

Fig. 3.

*H-3's bi-metallic strip, invented by Harrison before 1749, is composed of two thin strips of metal, one of brass (yellow), the other of steel (blue), riveted with one end fixed in the fiddle-shaped frame and the other with two pins that embrace the balance spring. When the temperature rises, the greater expansion of the brass bends the bi-metallic strip down, thereby reducing the effective length of the balance spring to compensate for its expansion and the change in its elasticity. When the temperature falls, the bi-metallic strip automatically makes the required adjustment in the opposite direction.*

One of the innovations Harrison introduced in H-3 can still be found today inside thermostats and other temperature-control devices. It is called, rather unpoetically, a bi-metallic strip. Like the gridiron pendulum, only better, the bi-metallic strip compensates immediately and automatically for any changes in temperature that could affect the clock's going rate. Although Harrison had done away with the pendulum in his first two sea clocks, he had maintained gridirons in their works, combining brass and steel rods mounted near the balances to render the clocks immune to temperature changes. Now, with H-3, he produced this simplified, streamlined strip—of fine sheet brass and steel riveted together—to accomplish the same end.

A novel antifriction device that Harrison developed for H-3 also survives to the present day—in the caged ball bearings that smooth the operation of almost every machine with moving parts now in use.

H-3, the leanest of the sea clocks, weighs only sixty pounds—fifteen pounds less than H-1 and twenty-six pounds lighter than H-2. In place of the dumbbell-shaped bar balances with their five-pound brass balls at either end, H-3 runs on two large, circular balances, mounted one above the other, linked by metal ribbons, and controlled by a single spiral spring.

Harrison had been aiming for compactness, mindful of the cramped quarters in a captain's cabin. He never considered trying to make a longitude *watch* to fit in the captain's pocket, because everyone knew that a watch could not possibly achieve the same accuracy as a clock. H-3, svelte in its dimensions of two feet high and one foot wide, had gone about as far as a sea clock could go toward diminution when Harrison completed the bulk of the work on it in 1757. Although he still wasn't altogether thrilled with its performance, Harrison deemed H-3 small enough to meet the definition of shipshape.

An odd coincidence—if you believe in coincidences—changed his thinking on that score. What with all the brass work and specialty detailing he required for the longitude timekeepers, Harrison had come to know and contract with various artisans in London. One of these was John Jefferys, a freeman of The Worshipful Company of Clockmakers. In 1753, Jefferys made Harrison a pocket watch for his personal use.

*John Harrison's pocket watch, made by John Jefferys in 1753, is the earliest surviving watch fitted both with maintaining power (to keep it running during winding) and temperature compensation (a bi-metallic strip). The dial shows the scars of World War II, when bombs struck a building in Hull where the watch was stored inside a safe.*

He obviously followed Harrison's design specifications, for Jefferys fitted the watch with a tiny bi-metallic strip to keep it beating true, come heat or cold. Other watches of the time sped up or slowed down by a factor of ten seconds for every one-degree change in temperature. And, whereas all previous watches either stopped dead or ran backward when they were being wound, this one boasted "maintaining power" that enabled it to keep running even through winding.

Some horologists consider the Jefferys timepiece the first true precision watch. Harrison's name is all over it, metaphorically speaking, but only John Jefferys signed it on the cap. (That it still exists, in the Clockmakers' Museum, is something of a miracle, since the watch lay inside a jeweler's safe in a shop that took a direct bomb hit during the Battle of Britain, then baked for ten days under the building's smoldering ruins.)

This watch proved remarkably dependable. Harrison's descendants recall that it was always in his pocket. It occupied his mind, too, shrinking his vision of the sea clock. He mentioned the Jefferys watch to the Board of Longitude in June of 1755, during one of

*At the Board of Longitude meeting on June 19, 1755, Harrison requested more funds for the completion of H-3 and for the construction of two watches, "one of such a size as may be worn in the Pocket & the other bigger." The latter was H-4. The former, which he later termed his "lesser" watch, is shown in this drawing. It is not known if this timekeeper was ever made.*

*The Parts here belonging to the Cycloid are too long*

his de rigueur explanations of the latest delay attending H-3. According to the minutes of that meeting, Harrison said he had "good reason to think," on the basis of a watch "already executed according to his direction"—i.e., the Jefferys watch—"that such small machines may be . . . of great service with respect to the longitude."

In 1759, when Harrison finished H-4, the timekeeper that ultimately won the longitude prize, it bore a stronger resemblance to the Jefferys watch than to any of its legitimate predecessors, H-1, H-2, or H-3.

Coming at the end of that big brass lineage, H-4 is as surprising as a rabbit pulled out of a hat. Though large for a pocket watch, at five inches in diameter, it is minuscule for a sea clock, and weighs only three pounds. Within its paired silver cases, a

RIGHT *Of the four designs for the decoration surrounding the chapter ring of H-4, Harrison selected the one at the top, as indicated in the instructions to the dial painter.*

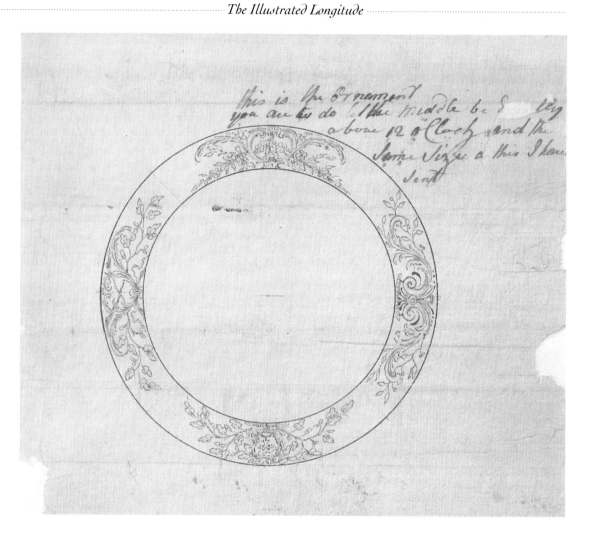

OPPOSITE *Harrison's prize-winning watch, H-4 (shown here at its actual size), was surprisingly small compared to his three earlier clocks. First mentioned at the Board of Longitude meeting in 1755, H-4 was completed in 1759 and tried at sea on two voyages, to Jamaica in 1761-62 and to Barbados in 1764.*

130

genteel white face shows off four fanciful repeats of a fruit-and-foliage motif drawn in black. These patterns ring the dial of Roman numeral hours and Arabic seconds, where three blued-steel hands point unerringly to the correct time. The Watch, as it soon came to be known, embodied the essence of elegance and exactitude.

Harrison loved it, and said so more clearly than he ever expressed another thought: "I think I may make bold to say, that there is neither any other Mechanical or Mathematical thing in the World that is more beautiful or curious in texture than this my watch or Timekeeper for the Longitude . . . and I heartily thank Almighty God that I have lived so long, as in some measure to complete it."

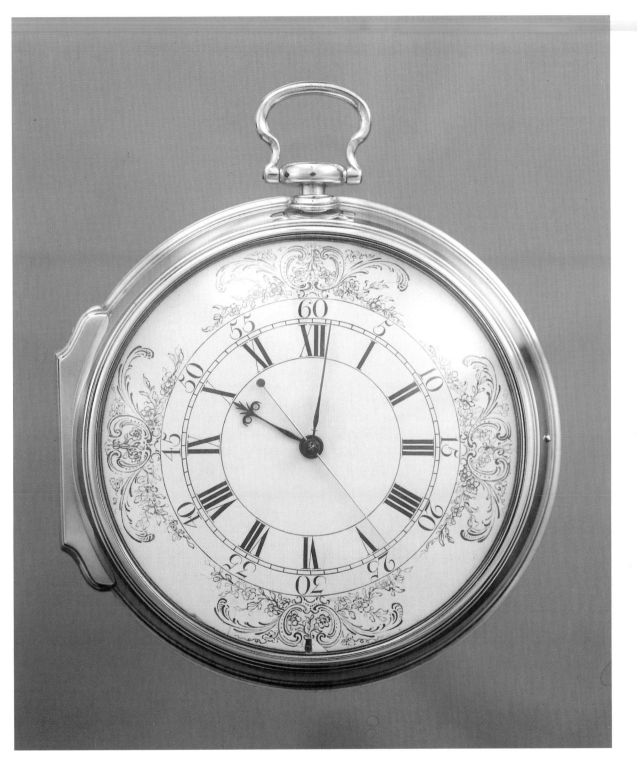

Inside this marvel, the parts look even lovelier than the face. Just under the silver case, a pierced and engraved plate protects the works behind a forest of flutings and flourishes. The designs serve no functional purpose other than to dazzle the beholder. A bold signature near the plate's perimeter reads "John Harrison & Son A.D. 1759." And under the plate, among the spinning wheels, diamonds and rubies do battle against friction. These tiny jewels, exquisitely cut, take over the work that was relegated to antifriction wheels and mechanical grasshoppers in all of Harrison's big clocks.

*No expense was spared in the finishing of H-4. The exquisite piercing and engraving of its backplate seem entirely appropriate for a timekeeper that represented the culmination of more than three decades of work and was destined to become one of the most famous watches of all time.*

How he came to master the jeweling of his Watch remains one of the most tantalizing secrets of H-4. Harrison's description of the watch simply states that "The pallets are diamonds." No explanation follows as to why he chose this material, or by what technique he shaped the gems into their crucial configuration. Even during the years when the Watch was dissected and inspected by committees of watchmakers and astronomers as it went through the mill of repeated trials, no recorded question or discussion came up regarding the diamond parts.

Lying in state now in an exhibit case at the National Maritime Museum, H-4 draws millions of visitors a year. Most tourists approach the Watch after having passed the cases containing H-1, H-2, and H-3. Adults and youngsters alike stand mesmerized before the big sea clocks. They move their heads to follow the swinging balances, which rock like metronomes on H-1 and H-2. They breathe in time to the regular rhythm of the ticking, and they gasp when startled by the sudden, sporadic spinning of the single-blade fan that protrudes from the bottom of H-2.

But H-4 stops them cold. It purports to be the end of some orderly progression of thought and effort, yet it constitutes a complete non sequitur. What's more, it holds still, in stark contrast to the whirring of the going clocks. Not only are its mechanisms hidden by the silver case enclosure, but the hands are frozen in time. Even the second hand lies motionless. H-4 does not run.

It *could* run, if curators would allow it to, but they demur, on the grounds that H-4 enjoys something of the status of a sacred relic or a priceless work of art that must be preserved for posterity. To run it would be to ruin it.

When wound up, H-4 goes for thirty hours at a time. In other words, it requires daily winding, just as the big sea clocks do. But unlike its larger predecessors, H-4 will not tolerate daily human intervention. Nay, H-4, often hailed as the most important timekeeper ever built, offers mute but eloquent testimony on this point, having suffered mistreatment at the hands of its own great popularity. As recently as fifty years ago, it lay in its original box, with the cushion and winding key. They have since been lost in the course of *using* H-4—transferring it from one place to another, exhibiting it, winding it, running it, cleaning it, transferring it again. In 1963, despite the sobering lesson of the lost box, H-4 visited the United States as part of an exhibition at the Naval Observatory in Washington.

Harrison's big sea clocks, like his tower clock at Brocklesby Park, have more wherewithal to withstand regular use because of their friction-free design features. They embody Harrison's pioneering work to eliminate friction through the careful selection and assembly of components. But even Harrison was unable to miniaturize the antifriction wheels and the caged roller bearings for the construction of H-4. As a result, he was forced to lubricate the watch.

The messy oil used for horological lubrication mandates scheduled maintenance (and this is as true today as it was in Harrison's time). As it seeps about the works, the oil changes viscosity and acidity, until it no longer lubricates but merely loiters in interior recesses, threatening to sabotage the machinery. To keep H-4 running, therefore, caretakers would have to clean it regularly, approximately once every three years, which would require the complete dismantling of all parts—and incur risk that some of the parts, no matter how carefully held with tweezers and awe, would be damaged.

Then, too, moving parts subjected to constant friction eventually wear out, even if they are kept lubricated, and then have to be replaced. Estimating the pace of this natural process of attrition, curators suppose that within three or four centuries, H-4 would become a very different object from the one Harrison bequeathed to us three centuries ago. In its present state of suspended animation, however, H-4 may look forward to a well-preserved life of undetermined longevity. It is expected to endure for hundreds of years, if not thousands—a future befitting the timepiece described as the *Mona Lisa* or *The Night Watch* of horology.

OPPOSITE *On January 24, 1963, about 200 years after its second trial to Barbados, H-4 left the shores of England for a third journey, this time aboard H.M.S. Lowestoft, which sailed from Portsmouth bound for Norfolk, Virginia. Upon arrival, H-4 was taken to the British Embassy in Washington, D.C., where, on March 8, it was presented by the British Ambassador to the U.S. Secretary of the Navy for exhibition at the U.S. Naval Observatory. H-4 was kept running throughout this year-long exhibition, which focused on the achievements of John Harrison. On May 3, 1964, it was placed aboard H.M.S. Adamant at New London, Connecticut, and arrived back in England at Devonport, near Plymouth, on May 21.*

## CHAPTER ELEVEN

# Trial by Fire and Water

Two lunar months are past, and more,
Since of these heroes half a score
Set out to try their strength and skill,
And fairly start for Flamsteed-Hill . . .
But take care, Rev. M-sk-l-n,
Thou scientific harlequin,
Nor think, by jockeying, to win....
For the *great donor* of the prize
Is just, as *Jove* who rules the skies.

"C.P." "Greenwich Hoy!" or "The Astronomical Racers"

A STORY THAT HAILS a hero must also hiss at a villain—in this case, the Reverend Nevil Maskelyne, remembered by history as "the seaman's astronomer."

In all fairness, Maskelyne is more an antihero than a villain, probably more hardheaded than hard-hearted. But John Harrison hated him with a passion, and with good reason. The tension between these two men turned the last stretch of the quest for the longitude prize into a pitched battle.

Maskelyne took up, then embraced, then came to personify the lunar distance method. The man and the method melded easily, for Maskelyne, who put off marrying until he was fifty-two, enslaved himself to accurate observation and careful calculation. He kept records of everything, from astronomical positions to events in his personal life (including each expenditure, large or small, over the course of four-score years), and noted them all with the same detached matter-of-factness. He even wrote his own auto-biography in the third person: "Dr. M.," this surviving handwritten volume begins, "is

*When this portrait was painted in 1785, Nevil Maskelyne (1732-1811) was fifty-three and had been astronomer royal for twenty years. During his long term in office he did much for the recognition of the Royal Observatory and for celestial navigation by originating the annual publication of the Nautical Almanac. His ardent belief in the lunar distance method, however, made him John Harrison's nemesis during the second trial of H-4, and his appointment as astronomer royal in 1765 placed him between Harrison and the balance of the £20,000 prize.*

the last male heir of an ancient family long settled at Purton in the County of Wilts." On subsequent pages, Maskelyne refers to himself alternately as "he" and "Our Astronomer"—even before his main character becomes astronomer royal in 1765.

The fourth in a long line of Nevils, Maskelyne was born on October 5, 1732. This made him about forty years younger than John Harrison, although he seemed never to have been *young*. Described by a biographer early on as "rather a swot" and "a bit of a prig," he threw himself into the study of astronomy and optics with every intention of becoming an important scientist. Family letters refer to his older brothers, William and Edmund, as "Billy" and "Mun," and call his younger sister, Margaret, "Peggy," but Nevil was always and only Nevil.

Unlike John Harrison, who had no formal education, Nevil Maskelyne attended Westminster School and Cambridge University. He worked his way through college, performing menial tasks in exchange for reduced tuition. As a fellow of Trinity College, he also took holy orders, which earned him the title of Reverend, and he served for a while as curate of the church at Chipping Barnet, roughly ten miles north of London. Sometime in the 1750s, while Maskelyne was still a student, his lifelong devotion to astronomy and his Cambridge connections brought him into the company of James Bradley, the third astronomer royal. They made a natural pair, and mated their two true methodical minds for life, in joint pursuit of a longitude solution.

Bradley, at this point in his career, was on the verge of codifying the lunar distance method with the help of the tables sent over from Germany by the astronomer-mathematician-mapmaker Tobias Mayer. Between 1755 and 1760, according to Maskelyne's account of the story, Bradley undertook 1,200 observations at Greenwich, followed by "laborious calculations" comparing them to Mayer's predictions, in an effort to verify the tables.

Maskelyne naturally took an interest in these matters. In 1761, on the occasion of the much-heralded astronomical event called the transit of Venus, Maskelyne won from Bradley a plum position on an expedition to prove the validity of Mayer's work—and to demonstrate the value of the tables for navigation.

Maskelyne voyaged to the tiny island of St. Helena, south of the Atlantic Equator, where Edmond Halley had journeyed in the previous century to map the southern stars, and where Napoleon Bonaparte would be condemned, in the following century, to live out his last days. Sailing to and from St. Helena, Maskelyne used Hadley's quadrant and Mayer's tables to find his longitude at sea, many times over, much to his and Bradley's delight. The lunar distance technique worked like a charm in Maskelyne's able hands.

Maskelyne also used lunar distances to establish the precise longitude of St. Helena, which had not been known before.

During his sojourn on the island, Maskelyne carried out what was ostensibly his primary mission: He watched over a period of hours as the planet Venus moved, like a small, dark blemish, across the sun's face. In order for Venus to transit, or trespass in this fashion, the planet must pass precisely between the Earth and the sun. Because of the relative positions and paths of the three bodies, transits of Venus come in pairs, one transit eight years after the other—but only a single pair per century.

Halley had witnessed part of a more common transit of Mercury from St. Helena in 1677. Very excited about the possibilities of such occurrences, he urged the Royal Society to track the next transit of Venus, which, like the return of Halley's comet, he could not possibly live long enough to see firsthand. Halley argued convincingly that lots of careful observations of the transit, taken from widely separated points on the globe, would reveal the actual distance between the Earth and the sun.

Thus, Maskelyne set out for St. Helena in January 1761 as part of a small but global scientific armada, which included numerous French astronomical excursions to carefully selected observing sites in Siberia, India, and South Africa. The June 6, 1761, transit of Venus also paired (Charles) Mason with (Jeremiah) Dixon on a successful observing run at the Cape of Good Hope—several years before the two British astronomers drew their famous boundary line between Pennsylvania and Maryland. The second transit, predicted for June 3, 1769, launched the first voyage of Captain James Cook, who proposed to view the event from Polynesia.

Maskelyne discovered that the weather at St. Helena, unfortunately, had not improved much since Halley's visit, and he missed the end of the transit behind a cloud. Nevertheless, he stayed on for many months, comparing the force of gravity at St. Helena with that at Greenwich, trying to measure the distance to the nearby bright star Sirius, and using observations of the moon to gauge the size of the Earth. This work, coupled with his prowess on the longitude frontier, more than made up for his problems in viewing Venus.

Meanwhile, another voyage of monumental importance to the longitude story, though altogether unrelated to the transit expeditions, also set sail in 1761, when William Harrison carried his father's watch on a sea trial to Jamaica.

Harrison's first timekeeper, H-1, had ventured only as far as Lisbon, Portugal, and H-2 had never gone to sea at all. H-3, almost twenty years in the making, might have been tried on the ocean immediately upon its completion in 1759 but for the inconvenience of the Seven Years War. This worldwide war spanned three continents, including North America, as it brought England, France, Russia, and Prussia, among other countries, into its fray. During the turmoil, Astronomer Royal Bradley had tested written copies of the lunar distance tables aboard warships patrolling the enemy coast of France. No one in his right mind, however, would send a one-of-a-kind instrument like H-3 into such troubled waters, where it might be captured by hostile forces. At least that was the argument Bradley gave in the beginning. But the argument fell apart in 1761, when the official trial of H-3 finally came up—despite the fact that the great war still raged, having progressed through only five of its eponymous seven years. It's irresistible to imagine that, by then, Bradley *wanted* something bad to happen to H-3. In any case, the international drive to pursue the transit of Venus must somehow have legitimized all voyages flying under the flag of science.

Between the completion and the trial date of H-3, Harrison had proudly presented his pièce de résistance, H-4, to the Board of Longitude in the summer of 1760. The Board opted to test both H-3 and H-4 together on the same voyage. Accordingly, in May of 1761, William Harrison sailed with the heavy sea clock, H-3, from London to the port of Portsmouth, where he had orders to wait for a ship assignment. John

*Portsmouth harbor, shown here at about the time of the trial of H-4, was one of England's largest, most secure, and best-fortified harbors. William Harrison departed from here with H-4 on its trial voyage to Jamaica in November 1761. Before embarking, the watch was set to the local time at the meridian of Portsmouth Naval Academy's observatory.*

Harrison, fussing and fine-tuning H-4 till the very last minute, planned to meet William at Portsmouth and deliver the portable timekeeper into his hands just before the ship weighed anchor.

Five months later, William was still on the dock in Portsmouth, waiting for his sailing orders. It was now October, and William fretted with frustration over the delayed trial and fear for the health of his wife, Elizabeth, still ill after the birth of their son, John.

William suspected that Dr. Bradley had deliberately delayed the trial for his personal gain. By holding up the Harrison trial, Bradley could buy time for Maskelyne to produce proof positive supporting the lunar distance method. This may sound like a paranoid delusion on William's part, but he had evidence of Bradley's own interest in the longitude prize. In a diary, William had recorded how he and his father chanced to encounter Dr. Bradley at an instrument-maker's shop, where they incurred his obvious antagonism: "The Doctor seemed very much out of temper," noted William, "and in the greatest passion told Mr. Harrison that if it had not been for him and his plaguey watch, Mr. Mayer and he should have shared Ten Thousand Pounds before now."

As astronomer royal, Bradley served on the Board of Longitude, and was therefore a judge in the contest for the longitude prize. This description of William's makes it sound as though Bradley himself was also a contender for the prize. Bradley's personal investment in the lunar distance method could be called a "conflict of interest," except that the term seems too weak to define what the Harrisons stood up against.

Whatever the cause of the delay, the Board convened to take action shortly after William returned to London in October, and November saw him embarked at last on H.M.S. *Deptford*. With H-4 alone. During the long predeparture delay, his father had seen fit to remove H-3 from the running. The Harrisons were banking everything on the Watch.

The board insisted, as a means of quality control over the trial, that the box containing H-4 be fitted with four locks, each opening to a different key. William got one of the keys, of course, for he had charge of the daily winding. The other three went to trusted men willing to witness William's every move—William Lyttleton, then governor-designate of Jamaica and William's fellow passenger aboard the *Deptford*, the ship's captain, Dudley Digges, and Digges's first lieutenant, J. Seward.

Two astronomers, one in Portsmouth and another one sailing along to Jamaica, took charge of establishing the correct local time of departure and arrival. William was required to set the Watch by them.

On the very first leg of the journey, much cheese and many whole barrels of drink were found unfit for consumption. Captain Digges ordered them thrown overboard, precipitating a crisis. "This day," reads a note in the journal of the ship's master, "all the Beer was expended, the People oblidged to drink water." William promised a speedy end to the distress, as he reckoned with H-4 that the *Deptford* would make Madeira

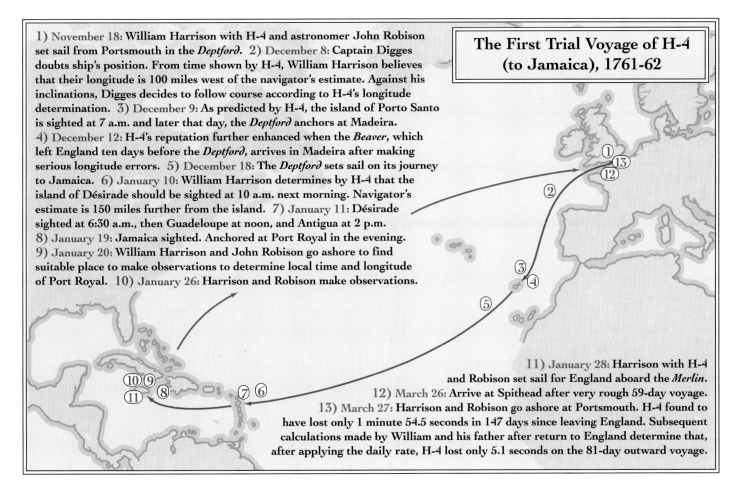

1) November 18: William Harrison with H-4 and astronomer John Robison set sail from Portsmouth in the *Deptford*. 2) December 8: Captain Digges doubts ship's position. From time shown by H-4, William Harrison believes that their longitude is 100 miles west of the navigator's estimate. Against his inclinations, Digges decides to follow course according to H-4's longitude determination. 3) December 9: As predicted by H-4, the island of Porto Santo is sighted at 7 a.m. and later that day, the *Deptford* anchors at Madeira. 4) December 12: H-4's reputation further enhanced when the *Beaver*, which left England ten days before the *Deptford*, arrives in Madeira after making serious longitude errors. 5) December 18: The *Deptford* sets sail on its journey to Jamaica. 6) January 10: William Harrison determines by H-4 that the island of Désirade should be sighted at 10 a.m. next morning. Navigator's estimate is 150 miles further from the island. 7) January 11: Désirade sighted at 6:30 a.m., then Guadeloupe at noon, and Antigua at 2 p.m. 8) January 19: Jamaica sighted. Anchored at Port Royal in the evening. 9) January 20: William Harrison and John Robison go ashore to find suitable place to make observations to determine local time and longitude of Port Royal. 10) January 26: Harrison and Robison make observations.

**The First Trial Voyage of H-4 (to Jamaica), 1761-62**

11) January 28: Harrison with H-4 and Robison set sail for England aboard the *Merlin*. 12) March 26: Arrive at Spithead after very rough 59-day voyage. 13) March 27: Harrison and Robison go ashore at Portsmouth. H-4 found to have lost only 1 minute 54.5 seconds in 147 days since leaving England. Subsequent calculations made by William and his father after return to England determine that, after applying the daily rate, H-4 lost only 5.1 seconds on the 81-day outward voyage.

within a day. Digges argued that the Watch was way off, as was the island, and offered to lay odds on the bet. Regardless, the next morning brought Madeira into sight—and fresh barrels of wine into the hold. At this juncture, Digges made Harrison a new offer: He would buy the first longitude timekeeper that William and his father put up for sale, the moment it became available. While still in Madeira, Digges wrote to John Harrison:

> Dear Sir, I have just time to acquaint you ... of the great perfection of your
>
> watch in making the island on the Meridian; According to our Log we were 1
>
> degree 27 minutes to the Eastward, this I made by a French map which lays down
>
> the longitude of Teneriffe, therefore I think your watch must be right. Adieu.

The Atlantic crossing took nearly three months. When the *Deptford* arrived at Port Royal, Jamaica, on January 19, 1762, the Board's representative John Robison set up his astronomical instruments and established local noon. Robison and Harrison then

*To determine local time by equal altitudes of the sun and longitude by the eclipses of Jupiter's satellites, an astronomer needed a temporary structure where the observations could be made. The construction of the observatory that William Harrison and John Robison used on Jamaica took six days, during which valuable observing time was lost. To avoid such delay, William Bayly, one of the astronomers on Cook's third voyage (1776-80), designed this portable observatory. The tent helped to protect the instruments from the elements; its roof, which was suspended from three logs lashed together, could be rotated as desired for observing.*

Plate.II.

synchronized their watches to fix the longitude of Port Royal by the time difference between them. H-4 had lost only five seconds—after 81 days at sea!

Captain Digges, a great one for giving credit where it was due, ceremonially presented William—and his father, in absentia—with an octant to commemorate the successful trial. Curators at the National Maritime Museum, where this particular trophy-instrument is now displayed, note on a comment card that it seems "an odd present, perhaps, for someone trying to make the Lunar-Distance Method of determining Longitude redundant." It must be the case that Captain Digges had seen a bullfight somewhere, and by this gesture he was awarding William the ears and tail of the vanquished animal. What's more, even with the Watch in hand to tell the time in London, Digges would still need his octant to establish local time at sea.

A little over a week after they reached Jamaica, William, Robison, and the Watch went back to England aboard the *Merlin.* With worse weather on the return, William worried constantly about keeping H-4 dry. The rough seas leapt onto the ship, often submerging the decks under two feet of water and leaking a good six inches into the captain's cabin. Here poor seasick William wrapped the Watch in a blanket for protection, and when the blanket got soaked, he slept in it to dry the cloth with his body heat. William ran a raging fever by the end of the voyage, thanks to these precautions, but felt vindicated by the result. Upon its arrival home on March 26, H-4 was still ticking. And its adjusted total error, outbound and homebound combined, amounted to just under two minutes.

The prize should have gone to John Harrison then and there, for his Watch had done all that the Longitude Act demanded, but events conspired against him and withheld the funds from his deserving hands.

*So impressed was Dudley Digges, the captain of the Deptford, by the performance of H-4 on the voyage to Jamaica, that he is reputed to have presented William Harrison with this commemorative relic of an octant, an instrument used not only for finding latitude but also for finding longitude by determining the local time of the ship. From the difference between the local time and the time of the home port, recorded by the marine timekeeper, the ship's longitude could easily be calculated.*

*On his voyage to and from the island of St. Helena off the west coast of Africa to observe the 1761 transit of Venus, Nevil Maskelyne claimed that he was able to determine longitude to within one degree using Tobias Mayer's lunar distance tables. Upon his return, Maskelyne published* The British Mariner's Guide, *which described his method of working and explained how to make the observations at sea.*

First there was the evaluation of the trial, which came up at the next meeting of the Board of Longitude, in June. Having stipulated the four keys and the two astronomers, the board now called for three mathematicians to check and recheck the data on the time determinations at Portsmouth and Jamaica, as both of these suddenly seemed insufficient and inaccurate. The commissioners also complained that William had failed to follow certain rules set down by the Royal Society for establishing the longitude at Jamaica by the eclipses of Jupiter's moons — something William didn't realize he was required to do, and wouldn't have known how to do in any case.

THE

Britiſh MARINER'S GUIDE.

CONTAINING,

Complete and Eaſy Inſtructions

FOR THE

Diſcovery of the LONGITUDE at Sea and Land, within a Degree, by Obſervations of the Diſtance of the Moon from the Sun and Stars, taken with HADLEY's Quadrant.

To which are added,

An APPENDIX, containing a Variety of intereſting Rules and Directions, tending to the Improvement of Practical Navigation in general.

And a Sett of correct

ASTRONOMICAL TABLES.

By NEVIL MASKELYNE, A.M.
Fellow of TRINITY COLLEGE, CAMBRIDGE, and of the ROYAL SOCIETY.

LONDON:
PRINTED for the AUTHOR;
And Sold by J. NOURSE, in the Strand; Meſſ. MOUNT and PAGE, on Tower-Hill; and Meſſ. HAWES, CLARKE, and COLLINS, in Pater-Noſter-Row.
M DCC LXIII.

Therefore, the board concluded in its final report in August 1762, "the Experiments already made of the Watch have not been sufficient to determine the Longitude at Sea." H-4 must needs submit to a new trial, under stricter scrutiny. Back to the West Indies with it, and better luck next time.

Instead of £20,000, John Harrison received £1,500, in recognition of the fact that his Watch "tho' not yet found to be of such great use for discovering the Longitude ... is nevertheless an invention of considerable utility to the Public." He could expect another £1,000 when H-4 returned from its second stint at sea.

Maskelyne, defender of the rival method, had arrived back in London from St. Helena in May 1762, hot on William's heels, and quite flush with accomplishment. He immediately cemented his future reputation by publishing *The British Mariner's Guide* — an English translation of Mayer's tables, plus directions for their use.

Mayer himself had died in February, at thirty-nine, the victim of a virulent infection. Then Bradley, the astronomer royal, died in July. His death, at sixty-nine, may have seemed less premature, though Maskelyne swore his mentor's life had been unduly shortened by hard labor on the lunar tables.

The Harrisons discovered immediately that the loss of Bradley from the Board of Longitude offered no reprieve. His death failed to soften the hard-nosed attitude of the other commissioners. All that summer, as the post of astronomer royal fell vacant and then was filled through the appointment of Nathaniel Bliss, William corresponded with the board members to vindicate the Watch. He took hard knocks at two board meetings in June and August, and carried the discouraging words home to his father.

*Nathaniel Bliss (1700-1764), the fourth astronomer royal, succeeded Halley as Savilian Professor of Geometry at Oxford when the latter died in 1742. The same influential backing that had elected him to that appointment led him to the post of astronomer royal in August 1762, after James Bradley's death. Bliss inspected the instruments that Maskelyne took with him on the voyage to Barbados for the second trial of H-4, but his tenure as astronomer royal was cut short by his unexpected death after only two years in office.*

As soon as Bliss took his ex officio seat on the Board of Longitude as the fourth astronomer royal, he took aim at the Harrisons. Like Bradley before him, Bliss was all for lunars. He insisted that the Watch's so-called accuracy was a mere chance occurrence, and he did not predict a precision performance on the next trial.

None of the astronomers or admirals on the board had any knowledge about the Watch or what made it run so regularly. They may have been incapable of understanding its mechanism, but they began hounding Harrison early in 1763 to explain it to them. This was a matter of both intellectual curiosity and national security. The Watch had value, for it seemed an improvement over the ordinary watches used to time the taking of lunars. The Watch might even stand in for the lunars in foul weather, when the moon and stars disappeared. Then, too, John Harrison wasn't getting any younger. What if he died and took the potentially useful secret to the grave

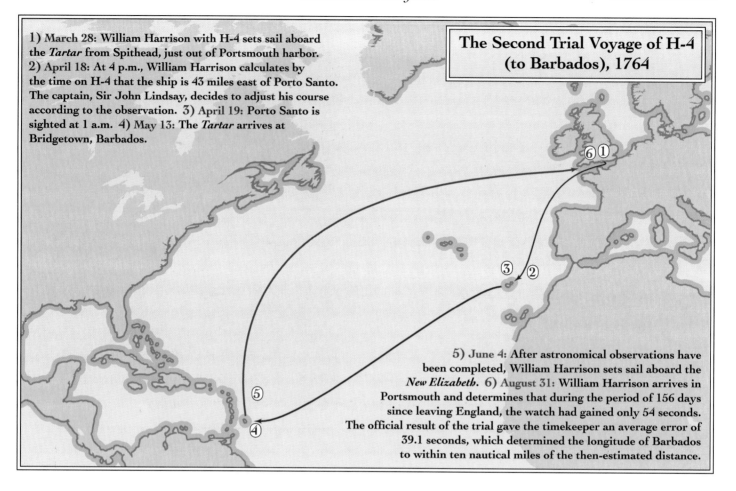

**The Second Trial Voyage of H-4 (to Barbados), 1764**

1) March 28: William Harrison with H-4 sets sail aboard the *Tartar* from Spithead, just out of Portsmouth harbor. 2) April 18: At 4 p.m., William Harrison calculates by the time on H-4 that the ship is 43 miles east of Porto Santo. The captain, Sir John Lindsay, decides to adjust his course according to the observation. 3) April 19: Porto Santo is sighted at 1 a.m. 4) May 13: The *Tartar* arrives at Bridgetown, Barbados.

5) June 4: After astronomical observations have been completed, William Harrison sets sail aboard the *New Elizabeth*. 6) August 31: William Harrison arrives in Portsmouth and determines that during the period of 156 days since leaving England, the watch had gained only 54 seconds. The official result of the trial gave the timekeeper an average error of 39.1 seconds, which determined the longitude of Barbados to within ten nautical miles of the then-estimated distance.

with him? What if William and the Watch went down together in some nautical disaster on the next trial? Clearly, the board needed a full disclosure on the timekeeper before they sent it back to sea.

The French government dispatched a small contingent of horologists, Ferdinand Berthoud among them, to London in the hope that Harrison would reveal the Watch's inner workings. Harrison, understandably wary by this time, shooed the French away, and begged his own countrymen to give him some assurance that no one would pirate his idea. He also asked Parliament for £5,000, to put teeth into their promise of protecting his rights. These negotiations quickly reached an impasse. No money and no information changed hands.

Finally, in March of 1764, William and his friend Thomas Wyatt boarded H.M.S. *Tartar* and sailed to Barbados with H-4. The *Tartar*'s captain, Sir John Lindsay, oversaw this first phase of the second trial, and monitored the handling of the Watch on the way to the West Indies. Arriving ashore on May 15, prepared to compare notes with the board-appointed astronomers who had preceded him to the island aboard the *Princess Louisa,* William found a familiar face. There at the observatory, standing ready to judge the performance of the Watch, was Nathaniel Bliss's handpicked henchman, none other than the Reverend Nevil Maskelyne.

Maskelyne was undergoing something of a second trial himself, he had complained to the locals. His lunar distance method had clearly shown itself the supreme solution to the longitude problem on the voyage to St. Helena. And this time, en route to Barbados, he boasted, he was sure he'd clinched the case and secured the prize.

When William heard word of these claims, he and Captain Lindsay challenged Maskelyne's fitness to judge H-4 impartially. Maskelyne was outraged by their accusations. He became huffy, then nervous. In his disquieted condition, he botched the astronomical observations—even though all those present recalled there wasn't a cloud in the sky.

## CHAPTER TWELVE

# A Tale of Two Portraits

How sour sweet music is
When time is broke and no proportion kept!
So is it in the music of men's lives.

I wasted time, and now doth time waste me;
For now hath time made me his numbering clock;
My thoughts are minutes.

WILLIAM SHAKESPEARE, *Richard II*

TWO COMPELLING LIKENESSES of John Harrison, both made during his lifetime, survive into ours. The first is a formal portrait in oils by Thomas King, completed sometime between October 1765 and May 1766. The other is an engraving by Peter Joseph Tassaert, from 1767, obviously taken from the painting, which it copies in almost every detail. In all details, really, except one—and this one difference tells a story of degradation and despair.

The painting now hangs in the gallery at the Old Royal Observatory. It shows Harrison as a man to be reckoned with. Dressed in a chocolate brown frock coat and britches, he sits surrounded by his inventions, including H-3 at his right and the precision gridiron-pendulum regulator, which he built to rate his other timepieces, behind him. Even seated he assumes an erect bearing and a look of self-satisfied, but not smug, accomplishment. He wears a gentleman's white wig and has the clearest, smoothest skin imaginable. (The story of Harrison's becoming fascinated with watchworks in childhood, while recuperating from an illness, holds that he suffered a severe

*John Harrison (1693-1776), was about seventy-three years old when he sat for this portrait by Thomas King. In his right hand is a pocket watch, probably the one made for him by John Jefferys in 1753, and behind him are two of his clocks, one symbolizing timekeeping on land, the other timekeeping at sea. The former is a regulator with his ingenious gridiron pendulum, the latter his third marine timekeeper (H-3).*

case of smallpox at the time. We must conclude, however, that the tale is tall, or that he experienced a miraculous recovery, or that the artist has painted out the scars.)

His blue eyes, though a bit rheumy at seventy-plus years of age, direct a level gaze. Only the eyebrows, raised at the center, and the lines between them, betray the man's cautious craftsmanship, his nagging concerns. He holds his left arm akimbo, hand on hip. His right forearm rests on a table, and in his fingers is . . . the Jefferys pocket watch!

*Where is H-4?* It was long finished by this time, and always the apple of his eye. Surely Harrison would have insisted on having it pose with him. Indeed, it *does* pose with him in the Tassaert engraving. Strange how the mezzotint departs from the oil at the point of Harrison's right wrist. His hand is empty in this image, upturned and vaguely gesturing toward the Watch, now lying on the table, a bit foreshortened by perspective, atop some drawings of itself. Admittedly, the timekeeper looks too large for Harrison to cradle comfortably in his palm, as he could do with the Jefferys watch, which was only half the size of H-4.

The reason H-4 is missing from the oil portrait is that Harrison didn't have it in his possession at the sittings. It was fudged in later, when Harrison's growing fame as "the man who found Longitude" occasioned the creation of the engraving. The intervening events stressed Harrison to the limits of his forbearance.

After the fractious second trial of the Watch in the summer of 1764, the Board of Longitude allowed months to pass without saying a word. The commissioners were waiting for the mathematicians to compare their computations of H-4's performance with the astronomers' observations of the longitude of Portsmouth and Barbados, all of which had to be factored into the judging. When they heard the final report, the commissioners conceded that they were "unanimously of opinion that the said timekeeper has kept its time with sufficient correctness." They could hardly say otherwise: The Watch proved to tell the longitude within ten miles—three times more accurately than the terms of the Longitude Act demanded! But this stupendous success gained Harrison only a small victory. The Watch and its maker still had lots of explaining to do.

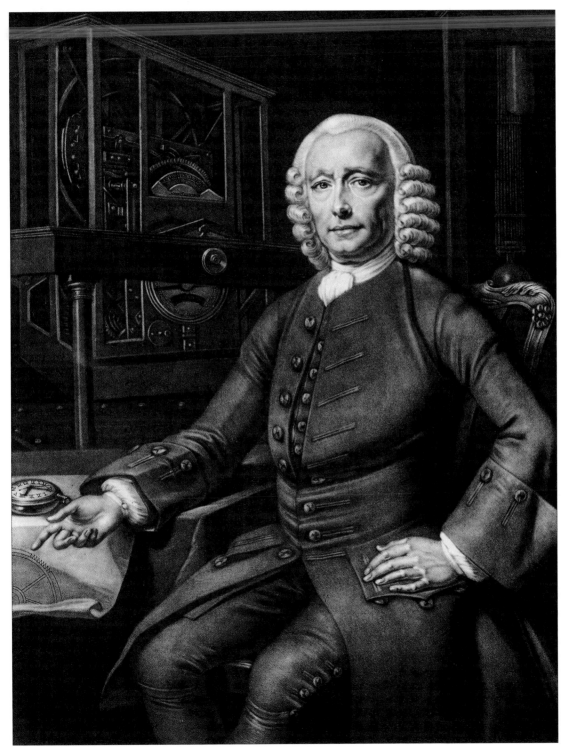

*In the mezzotint of John Harrison by Peter Joseph Tassaert, published in 1768, the handheld watch shown in King's portrait is replaced with the famous prize-winning watch, H-4, which lies on the table beside its celebrated maker.*

153

That autumn, the board offered to hand over *half* the reward money, on the condition that Harrison hand over to them all the sea clocks, plus a full disclosure of the magnificent clockwork inside H-4. If Harrison expected to receive the *full* amount of the £20,000 prize, then he would also have to supervise production of not one but *two* duplicate copies of H-4—as proof that its design and performance *could* be duplicated.

Adding to the tension of these developments, Nathaniel Bliss broke the long tradition of longevity associated with the title of astronomer royal. John Flamsteed had served in that capacity for forty years, Edmond Halley and James Bradley had each enjoyed a tenure of more than twenty, but Bliss passed away after just two years at the post. The name of the new astronomer royal—*and* ex officio member of the Board of Longitude—announced in January 1765, was, as Harrison no doubt predicted, his nemesis, Nevil Maskelyne.

The thirty-two-year-old Maskelyne took office as fifth astronomer royal on a Friday. The very next morning, Saturday, February 9, even before the ceremony of kissing the king's hand, he attended the scheduled meeting of the Board of Longitude as its newest commissioner. He listened while the thorny matter of Harrison's payment was further debated. He added his approval to the proposed monetary awards for Leonhard Euler and the widow of Tobias Mayer. Then Maskelyne attended to his own agenda.

He read aloud a long memorandum extolling the lunar distance method. A chorus of four captains from the East India Company, whom he'd brought with him, parroted these sentiments exactly. They had all used the procedure, many times, they said, just as it was outlined by Maskelyne in *The British Mariner's Guide*, and they always managed to compute their longitude in a matter of a mere four hours. They agreed with Maskelyne that the tables ought to be published and widely distributed, and then "this Method might be easily & generally practiced by Seamen."

This marked the beginning of a new groundswell in activity directed at institutionalizing the lunar distance method. Harrison's chronometer may have been quick, but it was still a quirk, while the heavens were universally available to all.

The year of 1765 brought Harrison further woes, in the form of a new longitude act from Parliament. This one—officially called Act 5 George III *cap.*20—put caveats and conditions on the original act of 1714, and included stipulations that applied specifically to Harrison. It even named him in the opening language and described the current status of his contrariety with the board.

Harrison's mood deteriorated. He stormed out of more than one board meeting, and was heard swearing that he would not comply with the outrageous demands foisted on him "so long as he had a drop of English blood in his body."

Lord Egmont, the chairman of the board, gave Harrison his comeuppance: "Sir . . . you are the strangest and most obstinate creature that I have ever met with, and, would you do what we want you to do, and which is in your power, I will give you my word to give you the money, if you will but do it[!]"

Eventually, Harrison knuckled under. He turned in his drawings. He provided a written description. He promised to bare all before a committee of experts chosen by the board.

Anno quinto

# Georgii III. Regis.

## C A P. XX.

An Act for explaining and rendering more effectual Two Acts, One made in the Twelfth Year of the Reign of Queen *Anne*, intituled, *An Act for providing a publick Reward for such Person or Persons as shall discover the Longitude at Sea;* and the other in the Twenty sixth Year of the Reign of King *George* the Second, intituled, *An Act to render more effectual an Act made in the Twelfth Year of the Reign of Her late Majesty Queen* Anne, *intituled,* An Act for providing a publick Reward for such Person or Persons as shall discover the Longitude at Sea, *with regard to the making Experiments of Proposals made for discovering the Longitude; and to enlarge the Number of Commissioners for putting in Execution the said Act.*

4 3 2                    𝔚𝔥𝔢𝔯𝔢𝔞𝔰

b

Later that summer, on August 14, 1765, this illustrious party arrived at Harrison's house in Red Lion Square for a watchmakers' tribunal. Present were two of the Cambridge math professors Harrison referred to derisively as "Priests" or "Parsons," the Reverend John Michell and the Reverend William Ludlam. Three reputable watchmakers attended: Thomas Mudge, a man keenly interested in making marine timekeepers himself, William Mathews, and Larcum Kendall, formerly apprentice to John Jefferys. The sixth committee man was the widely respected scientific instru-

OPPOSITE *The purpose of the* Nautical Almanac *was to facilitate the lunar distance method by providing tables that simplified the calculations. Indeed, it is estimated that the tables reduced the time involved from four hours to about half an hour. Nevil Maskelyne, who was responsible for their publication, remarked that with the* Nautical Almanac *"sailors will have little more to do than to observe carefully the moon's distance from the sun or a proper star" in order to determine longitude at sea. This was an exaggeration because, even with the tables, the calculations are tedious and subject to the arithmetical ability of the sailor. Furthermore, the method could not be used for several days around the time of a new moon. Nevertheless, the* Nautical Almanac *made the technique a practicable solution to the longitude problem, and, compared to the cost of chronometers at that time, the sextant and publications required for the lunar distance method were very inexpensive.*

ment maker John Bird, who had fitted the Royal Observatory with mural quadrants and transit instruments for mapping the stars, and outfitted many scientific expeditions with unique devices.

Nevil Maskelyne came along, too.

Over the course of the next six days, Harrison dismantled the Watch piece by piece, explained—under oath—the function of each part, described how the various innovations worked together to keep virtually perfect time, and answered all the questions put to him. When it was over, the judges signed a certificate saying that they believed Harrison had indeed told them everything he knew.

As the coup de grâce, the board insisted that Harrison now reassemble the Watch and surrender it, locked in its box, to be sequestered (held for ransom, really) in a storeroom at the Admiralty. At the same time, he had to commence building the two replicas—without the Watch to serve as a guiding pattern, and stripped even of his original diagrams and description, which Maskelyne had delivered to the print shop so they could be copied, engraved, published in book form, and sold to the public at large.

What a time to sit for a portrait. Yet it was at this juncture that Mr. King painted Mr. Harrison. A look of calm may have come over him late that autumn, when he at last received the £10,000 he had been promised by the board.

At the beginning of the New Year, 1766, Harrison heard for the second time from Ferdinand Berthoud, who arrived from Paris with high hopes of accomplishing what he had failed to do on his last trip in 1763: learn the details of H-4's construction. Harrison felt little inclined to confide in Berthoud. Why should he divulge his secrets to anyone who couldn't make him do so? Parliament had been willing to pay £10,000 to hear from Harrison what Berthoud seemed to expect for peanuts. On behalf of the French government, Berthoud offered £500 for a private tour of H-4. Harrison refused.

Berthoud, however, before coming to London, had been in correspondence, watchmaker to watchmaker, with Thomas Mudge. Now that Berthoud was in town, he dropped in at Mudge's shop in Fleet Street. Apparently, no one had told Mudge—or any of the other expert witnesses—that Harrison's disclosure was supposed to be kept confidential. In the course of dining with the visiting horologist, Mudge waxed loquacious on the subject of H-4. He had held it in his hands and been privy to the discovery of its most intimate details, all of which he shared with Berthoud. He even drew sketches.

As it turned out, Berthoud and the other continental clockmakers did not steal Harrison's designs in the construction of their own marine timekeepers. Yet Harrison had cause to cringe at the casual manner in which his case was opened and aired.

The Board of Longitude slapped Mudge's wrist. The commissioners were not overly upset by his indiscretion, and besides, they had a few other matters to oversee, in addition to the Harrison affair. Notable among these was the petition from the Reverend Mr. Maskelyne, who wanted to begin annual publication of the nautical ephemerides for seamen interested in finding longitude by lunars. By incorporating a wealth of prefigured data, he would reduce the number of arithmetical calculations the individual navigator had to make, and thereby dramatically shorten the time required to arrive at a position—from four hours to about thirty minutes. The astronomer royal declared himself more than willing to undertake responsibility for the work. All he needed from the board, as official publisher, was the funding to pay salaries for a pair of human computers who could hash out the mathematics, plus the printer's fees.

Maskelyne produced the first volume of the *Nautical Almanac and Astronomical Ephemeris* in 1766, and went on supervising it until his dying day. Even

THE

NAUTICAL ALMANAC

AND

ASTRONOMICAL EPHEMERIS,

FOR THE YEAR 1769.

Publiſhed by ORDER of the

COMMISSIONERS OF LONGITUDE.

LONDON:

Printed by W. RICHARDSON and S. CLARK, PRINTERS;
AND SOLD BY
J. NOURSE, in the Strand, and Meſſ. MOUNT and PAGE, on Tower-Hill,
Bookſellers to the ſaid COMMISSIONERS.
M DCC LXVIII.
[Price Two Shillings and Six Pence.]

*The distance of the moon from the sun and west of certain stars was calculated at three-hour intervals, based on the time at the meridian of the Royal Observatory at Greenwich, as shown in this example from the* Nautical Almanac *for August 1769. The* Nautical Almanac *was an invaluable tool for the navigator because, in addition to these tables, it provided all kinds of information required for celestial navigation. As a result of this publication, by 1879 about two-thirds of all the ships in the world (72 percent of the commercial tonnage) were using the Greenwich meridian as the prime meridian.*

after his death, in 1811, seamen continued relying on his work for an additional few years, since the 1811 edition contained predictions straight through to 1815. Then others took over the legacy, continuing the publication of the lunar tables until 1907, and of the *Almanac* itself up to the present time.

The *Almanac* represents Maskelyne's enduring contribution to navigation—and the perfect task for him, too, as it embodied an abundance of excruciating detail: He included twelve full pages of data for each month, abbreviated and in fine print, with the moon's position calculated every three hours vis-à-vis the sun or the ten guide stars. Everyone agreed, the *Almanac* and its companion volume, the *Tables Requisite*, provided the surest way for mariners to fix their positions at sea.

In April of 1766, after Harrison's portrait was completed, the board dealt him another blow that might well have changed his mien.

In order to put to rest all lingering doubts that H-4's accuracy might be chalked up to chance or luck, the board decided to subject the timekeeper to a new sort of trial, even more rigorous than the two voyages. To this end, the timekeeper was to be moved from the Admiralty to the Royal Observatory, where, for a period of ten months, it would undergo daily tests performed, in his official capacity, by the astronomer royal, Nevil Maskelyne. Also the large longitude machines (the three sea clocks) were to be consigned to Greenwich, and have their going rates compared with that of the big regulator clock at the Observatory.

Imagine Harrison's reaction when he learned that his treasure, H-4, having languished many months in a lonely tower at the Admiralty, had been delivered into the hands of his arch-enemy. Within days of this shock, he heard a knock at his door, and opened it to find Maskelyne, unannounced, carrying a warrant for the arrest of the sea clocks.

"Mr. John Harrison," this missive begins, "We the . . . Commissioners appointed by the Acts of Parliament for the discovery of the Longitude at Sea, do hereby require you to deliver up to the Rev. Nevil Maskelyne, Astronomer Royal at Greenwich, the three several Machines or Timekeepers, now remaining in your hands, which are become the property of the public."

Cornered, Harrison led Maskelyne into the room where he kept the clocks, which had been his close companions for thirty years. They were all running, each in its own characteristic way, like a gathering of old friends in animated conversation. Little did they care that time had rendered them obsolete. They chattered on among themselves, oblivious to the world at large, lovingly cared for in this cozy place.

# TABLES

REQUISITE TO BE USED WITH THE

## NAUTICAL EPHEMERIS

FOR FINDING THE

### LATITUDE AND LONGITUDE AT SEA.

PUBLISHED BY ORDER OF THE

### COMMISSIONERS OF LONGITUDE.

*By Nevil Maskelyne.*

THE SECOND EDITION,

CORRECTED AND IMPROVED.

LONDON:

PRINTED BY WILLIAM RICHARDSON IN THE STRAND;

AND SOLD BY

C. NOURSE in the STRAND, and Meff. MOUNT and PAGE on TOWER-HILL,

BOOKSELLERS to the faid COMMISSIONERS.

MDCCLXXXI.

*Tables Requisite, the companion volume to the Nautical Almanac, provided information that did not vary from year to year, such as mathematical tables for computing latitude and longitude by observation. In 1767, Nevil Maskelyne printed 10,000 copies of the first edition, all of which had been sold by 1780. The second edition, with revisions and corrections, appeared in the following year.*

*This view of the Royal Observatory from the southeast was painted around 1766, the time when Nevil Maskelyne brought John Harrison's first three marine timekeepers to Greenwich. When Jean Bernoulli visited there in 1769, one of Harrison's timekeepers was in the library and another in the mural quadrant room. Soon after Harrison died in 1776, the three large machines were removed to storage, where they slowly deteriorated.*

James Tassie's enamel paste portrait of John Harrison, c. 1775, is one of only two examples of this model known to have survived.

Before parting with his sea clocks, Harrison wanted Maskelyne to grant him one concession—to sign a written statement that the timekeepers were in perfect order when he found them under Harrison's roof. Maskelyne argued, then acceded that they were *by all appearances* in perfect order, and affixed his signature. Anger escalated on both sides, so that when Maskelyne asked Harrison how to transport the timekeepers (i.e., should they be moved as is, or partly dismantled), Harrison sulked and intimated that any advice he gave would surely be used against him in the event of some mishap. At length he offered that H-3 might go as it was, but that H-1 and H-2 needed to be taken apart a bit. He could not watch this ignominy, however, and went upstairs to be alone in his private room. From there, he heard the crash on the ground floor. Maskelyne's workers, while carrying H-1 outside to the waiting cart, *dropped* it. By accident, of course.

Although H-4 had traveled on a boat, accompanied by Larcum Kendall, down the Thames to Greenwich for its trial, the three large sea clocks rumbled and bumped their way there through the streets of London in an unsprung cart. We need not imagine Harrison's response. The enamel paste medallion portrait of him in profile by James Tassie depicts the aging watchmaker's thin lips decidedly downturned.

Capt: James Cook
of the Endeavour.

## CHAPTER THIRTEEN

# The Second Voyage of Captain James Cook

When the greatest of England's bold voyagers perished,
'Twas the ear of a savage that heard his last groans
And, far from the land where his memory is cherished,
On a tropical island are scattered his bones:
[Un]just was the fate that arrested his motion,
Who with vigour unequalled, unyielding devotion,
Surveyed every coast, and explained every ocean,
In frigid, and torrid, and temperate zones.

GEORGE B. AIRY (Sixth Astronomer Royal) "Dolcoath"

SAUERKRAUT.

That was the watchword on Captain James Cook's triumphant second voyage, which set sail in 1772. By adding generous portions of the German staple to the diet of his English crew (some of whom foolishly turned up their noses at it), the great circumnavigator kicked scurvy overboard. Not only is sauerkraut's chief ingredient, cabbage, loaded with vitamin C but the fine-cut cabbage must be salted and allowed to ferment until sour to be worthy of the name. Practically pickled in brine, sauerkraut keeps forever aboard ship—or at least as long as the duration of a voyage around the world. Cook made it his oceangoing vegetable, and sauerkraut went on saving sailors' lives until lemon juice and, later, limes replaced it in the provisions of the Royal Navy.

With his men properly nourished, Cook had all hands available to carry out scientific experiments and explorations. He also conducted field tests for the Board of

*James Cook (1728-79) joined the Royal Navy when he was twenty-seven and in four years rose to the rank of master. He soon gained a reputation as an astronomer and surveyor and was chosen by the Royal Society in 1768 to lead an expedition to Tahiti to observe the transit of Venus on June 3, 1769. Cook (now a lieutenant) went on to survey the coast of New Zealand and the east coast of Australia. The success of this expedition resulted in his second voyage of exploration and discovery to the South Seas, this time to resolve the question of the existence of a great southern continent.*

Longitude, comparing the lunar distance method, which Cook was mariner enough to master, with several new sea clocks modeled after John Harrison's marvelous timekeeper.

"I must here take note," Cook wrote in his journal of the *Resolution*'s voyage, "that indeed our error (in Longitude) can never be great, so long as we have so good a guide as [the] watch."

Harrison had wanted Cook to take along the original H-4, not a copy or an imitation. He would gladly have gambled the balance of his reward money and let the win or loss of the second £10,000 ride on the Watch's performance under Cook's command. But the Board of Longitude said that H-4 would have to stay at home within the kingdom until its status regarding the remainder of the longitude prize had been decided.

Remarkably enough, H-4, which had sailed through two sea trials, won plaudits from three captains, and even earned a testimonial to its accuracy from the Board of Longitude, had *failed* its ten-month trial at the Royal Observatory between May 1766 and March 1767. Its going rate had gone erratic, so that it sometimes gained as many as twenty seconds a day. This may have been the unfortunate result of damage from the dismantling of H-4 during the disclosure proceedings. Some say Nevil Maskelyne's ill will hexed the Watch, or that he handled it roughly during daily winding. Others avow that he intentionally distorted the trial.

There is something odd about the logic Maskelyne used to gather his damning statistics. He pretended that the timekeeper was making six voyages to the West Indies, each of six weeks' duration—harking back to the original terms of the Longitude Act of 1714, which was still in effect. Maskelyne made no allowance for the fact that the Watch seemed to have incurred some damage, which showed in the way it now over-reacted mercurially to temperature changes, instead of acclimating smoothly and accurately, as had been its hallmark in the past. Regardless, Maskelyne just tallied up its performance statistics on each "voyage," while H-4 lay bolted to a window seat in the Observatory. Then he translated its gain in time into degrees of longitude, and from there into a distance expressed in nautical miles at the Equator. On its first mock trip, for example, H-4 gained thirteen minutes and twenty seconds, or 3 degrees, 20 minutes of longitude, and so missed the mark by two hundred nautical miles. It did slightly better on the ensuing sallies, and had its best run on the fifth try, when it shot only eighty-five miles wide of its desired landfall, having gained five minutes and forty-seconds, or 1 degree and 25 minutes of longitude. Thus Maskelyne was forced to conclude, "That Mr. Harrison's watch cannot be depended upon to keep the Longitude within a degree in a West India voyage of six weeks."

Previous records proved, however, that Mr. Harrison's watch had already kept the longitude to within *half* a degree or better on two *actual* voyages to the West Indies.

Yet Maskelyne was saying the Watch could not be trusted to keep track of a ship's position on a six-week voyage "nor to keep the longitude within half a degree for more than a few days; and perhaps not so long, if the cold be very intense; nevertheless, that it is a useful and valuable invention, and, in conjunction with the observations of the distance of the moon from the sun and fixed stars, may be of considerable advantage to navigation."

With these words of faint praise, Maskelyne tactfully conceded a few major flaws in the lunar distance method. To wit: For about six days of every month, the moon is so close to the sun that it disappears from view, and no lunar distance measurements whatever can be made. At such times, H-4 would indeed "be of considerable advantage to navigation." A timekeeper would also come in quite handy during the thirteen days per month when the moon lights up the night and lies on the other side of the world

OPPOSITE *One of the instructions given to Cook on his second voyage was to test the performance of four timekeepers, three by John Arnold and the other an exact copy of H-4 made by Larcum Kendall (K-1). An extract from the winding and comparison records of Arnold No. 3 and K-1, which were used aboard the* Resolution, *is shown here. The watches were wound and compared every day at noon, in the presence of Cook, the astronomer William Wales, and the first lieutenant Robert Cooper. Although Arnold's timekeeper did not run well, K-1 became their dependable guide.*

*167*

from the sun. Unable to measure the huge distance between the two big bodies for these two weeks, navigators plotted the moon against the fixed stars. They checked the times of their night observations on an ordinary watch, which might not be accurate enough to make the game worth the candle. With a timekeeper like H-4 aboard, the lunars could be precisely fixed in time and made more dependable. Thus, in his opinion, the timekeeper might enhance the lunar distance method but never supplant it.

In sum, Maskelyne airily deemed the Watch to be less constant than the stars.

Harrison issued a hailstorm of objections in a sixpenny booklet published at his own expense—though doubtless with the help of a ghost writer, since the diatribe is written in clear, plain English. One of his claims attacked the men who were supposed to witness Maskelyne's daily interactions with the Watch. These individuals resided in the nearby Royal Greenwich Hospital, an institution for seamen no longer fit for active duty. Harrison charged that the ex-sailors were too old and wheezy to climb the steep hill up to the Observatory. Even if they had enough breath and limbs to reach the summit, he argued, they dared not gainsay the astronomer royal in any of his actions but just signed their names in the register, seconding whatever Maskelyne wrote.

What's more, Harrison complained, H-4 had been situated in direct sunlight. Secured as it was inside a box with a glass cover, the Watch endured the same stifling heat as in a greenhouse. Meanwhile, the thermometer for measuring the timekeeper's ambient temperature lay on the other side of the room—in the shade.

Maskelyne felt no compunction to answer any of these allegations. He never spoke to either of the Harrisons again, nor they to him.

168

Harrison expected a reunion with H-4 after it had run Maskelyne's gauntlet. He asked the Board of Longitude if he could have it back. The Board declined. The seventy-four-year-old Harrison had to proceed with the making of his two new watches on the strength of his past experience and memories of H-4. The board gave him, in the way of further guidance, a couple of copies of the book containing Harrison's own drawings and description, which Maskelyne had recently published, titled *The Principles of Mr. Harrison's Timekeeper with Plates of the Same*. The whole intent of this book, after all, was to enable *anyone* to reconstruct H-4. (In truth, the description, since Harrison wrote it, utterly defied understanding.)

Seeking proof positive of H-4's true reproducibility, the board also hired the watchmaker Larcum Kendall to attempt an exact copy. These efforts evince the board's ferocious pursuit of the *spirit* of the law as they interpreted it, for the original Longitude Act never stipulated that the "Practicable and Useful" method must be copied by its inventor or anyone else.

Kendall, a man known to Harrison and respected by him, had been John Jefferys's apprentice. He may have lent a hand in the construction of the Jefferys pocket watch and even of H-4. He had also served as one of the expert witnesses at the exhaustive six-day "discovery" of H-4. In short, he was the perfect person to produce the replica. Even Harrison thought so.

Kendall finished his reproduction after two and a half years' work. Receiving K-1 in January of 1770, the Board of Longitude reconvened the committee that had scrutinized H-4, for these men would be the best judges of how closely the one resembled the other. Accordingly, John Michell, William Ludlam, Thomas Mudge, William Mathews, and John Bird met to examine K-1. Kendall absented himself this time, as was only fitting. His vacant seat on the panel was filled, naturally enough, by William Harrison. The consensus deemed K-1 a dead ringer for H-4—except that it had an even greater abundance of curlicue flourishes engraved on the backplate where Kendall signed his name.

OPPOSITE *William Wales (1734-98) served as the astronomer aboard the* Resolution *on Cook's second voyage. Prior to serving under Cook, he had been sent by the Royal Society to observe the 1769 transit of Venus on the northwest coast of Hudson's Bay. While waiting for the transit, he amused himself by calculating tables showing the equations of equal altitudes, in order to make it easier to determine local time. These tables were first published in the* Nautical Almanac *for 1773. Wales was elected a Fellow of the Royal Society in 1776. Like Cook, he was an expert in determining longitude by the lunar distance method, but after the second voyage, he became a strong supporter of the timekeeper method. In 1794, the same year in which this portrait was made, Wales published a book entitled* The Method of Finding Longitude by Timekeepers.

*169*

*Larcum Kendall's first marine timekeeper (K-1), the exact copy of H-4, cost the Board of Longitude £500. K-1's performance on Captain Cook's second voyage to the South Pacific, the most arduous trial to which it could have been subjected, proved that a marine timekeeper provided the most practicable method of finding longitude at sea. The movement of K-1 (RIGHT) shows Larcum Kendall's exquisite workmanship. Kendall was apprenticed to John Jefferys (who made Harrison's pocket watch, the forerunner to H-4) and worked as an escapement maker for George Graham. Harrison, who may have employed Kendall in the construction of H-4, must have thought very highly of his ability, because he agreed that Kendall should be the one to make the exact copy of H-4. Kendall was also the one chosen to repair H-1 after it was dropped during its removal from Harrison's workshop in 1766.*

William Harrison, lavish with his praise, told the board that in some respects Kendall's workmanship proved superior to his father's. He must have wished he could eat those words later, when the Board selected K-1 over H-4 to sail the Pacific with Captain Cook.

The board's decision had nothing to do with which was the better watch, for it viewed H-4 and K-1 as identical twins. It was just that the board had grounded H-4. So Cook took the K-1 copy on his world tour, along with three cheaper imitations offered by an upstart chronometer maker named John Arnold.

Harrison, meanwhile, by 1770—despite his ill treatment, advanced age, failing eyesight, and periodic bouts of gout—had finished building the first of the two watches the board had ordered him to make. This timekeeper, now known as H-5, has all the internal complexity of H-4 but assumes an austere outward appearance. No frills adorn its dial. The small brass starburst in the center of the face seems somewhat ornamental, like a tiny flower with eight petals. Actually, it's a knurled knob that pierces the glass cover on the dial; turning it sets the hands without lifting that glass, and so helps keep dust out of the movement.

*H-5, Harrison's fifth marine timekeeper, shown here in its original box, represents a further development of his work on marine timekeepers rather than being simply a duplication of H-4.*

The inscription, "No. 2 John Harrison and Son London 1770," on the backplace of H-5 indicates that this was Harrison's second longitude watch. H-5 is elegant and beautifully made, but it does not have the elaborate and expensive finish found on the backplate of H-4. Its purpose was only to meet the demands of accuracy required, and this it accomplished. After a ten-week trial at the king's observatory, the watch gained only 4.5 seconds.

Harrison perhaps intended the star-flower as a subliminal message. Since it recalls the position and shape of a compass rose, it conjures up that other, more ancient instrument, the magnetic compass, that sailors trusted for so long to find their way.

The backplate of H-5 looks barren and bland compared to the exuberant frippery scrolled over the same part of H-4. Indeed, H-5 is the work of a sadder but wiser man, compelled to do what he had once done willingly, even joyfully. Still, H-5 is a thing of beauty in its simplicity. It now occupies center stage at the Clockmakers' Museum in Guildhall, London, literally in the very middle of the room, where it rests on the frayed, red satin cushion inside its original wooden box.

Having built this watch in three years, Harrison tested and adjusted it for another two. By the time it pleased him, he was seventy-nine. He did not see how he could now start another project of equal proportions. Even if he were able to complete the work, the official trials might extend into the next decade, though his life surely could not. This sense of being backed against the wall, without hope of justice, emboldened him to tell his troubles to the king.

His Majesty King George III took an active interest in science, and had followed the trials of H-4. He had even granted John and William Harrison an audience when H-4 returned from its first voyage to Jamaica. More recently, King George had opened a private observatory at Richmond, just in time to view the 1769 transit of Venus.

In January 1772, William wrote the king a poignant letter covering the history of his father's hardships with the Board of Longitude and the Royal Observatory. William asked politely, beseechingly, if the new Watch (H-5) might "be lodged for a certain time in the Observatory at Richmond, in order to ascertain and manifest its degree of excellence."

The king then interviewed William at length at Windsor Castle. In a later account of this pivotal meeting, written in 1835 by William's son, John, the king is reported to have muttered under his breath, "These people have been cruelly treated." Aloud he promised William, "By God, Harrison, I will see you righted!"

True to his word, George III turned H-5 over to his private science tutor and Observatory director, S.C.T. Demainbray, for a six-week indoor trial, reminiscent of Maskelyne's modus operandi. As in previous sea and land trials, H-5's box was locked and three keys distributed among the three principals: one for Dr. Demainbray, one for William, and one for King George. The men met each day at noon in the observatory to check the watch against the regulator clock and then rewind it.

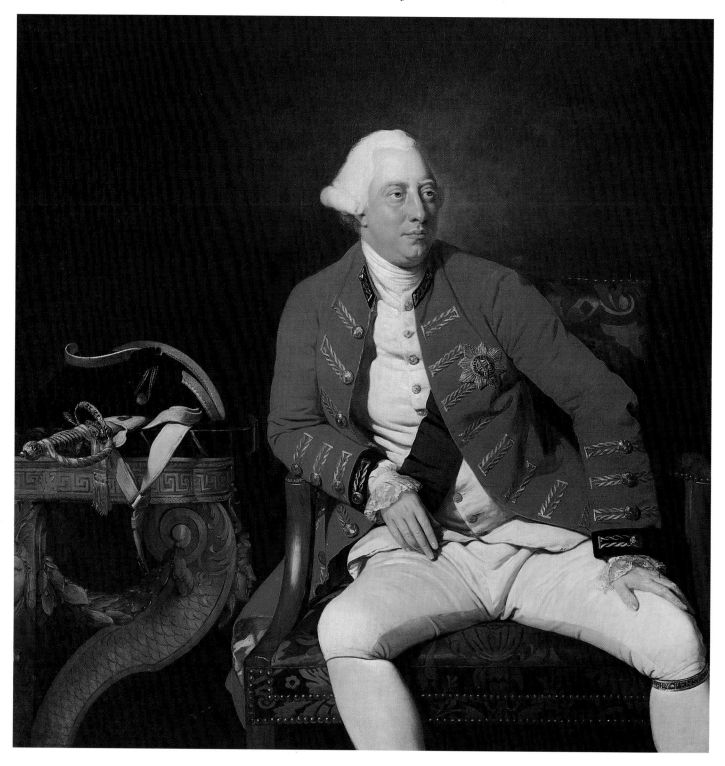

The watch, despite this reverential treatment, behaved badly at first. It gained and lost with abandon, crushing the Harrisons with embarrassment. Then the king recalled that he'd stored a few lodestones in a closet near the watch station, and he himself rushed to retrieve them. Freed from the stones' strange attraction to its parts, H-5 regained its composure and lived up to expectations.

The king extended the period of the trial in anticipation of objections from the Harrisons' enemies. After ten weeks of daily observations between May and July 1772, he felt proud to defend this new timekeeper, for H-5 had proved accurate to within one-third of one second per day.

He took the Harrisons under his aegis and helped them circumvent the obdurate board, by appealing directly to the prime minister, Lord North, and to Parliament for "bare justice," as William called it.

With the government badgering the board, the longitude commissioners met on April 24, 1773, to trace the whole tortuous course of the Harrison case yet again, in front of two witnesses from Parliament. Then Harrison's particulars came up for debate in Parliament three days later. At the king's suggestion, Harrison dropped his legal blustering and simply appealed to the hearts of the ministers. He was an old man. He had devoted his life to these endeavors. And although he had succeeded, he was rewarded with only half a prize plus new—and impossible—demands.

This approach carried the day. The final resolution took a few more weeks to go through channels, but at last, at the end of June, Harrison received £8,750. This amount nearly totaled the remainder of the longitude prize due him, but it was *not* the coveted prize. Rather, the sum was a bounty awarded by the benevolence of Parliament—in spite of the Board of Longitude, instead of from it.

Soon another act of Parliament laid out the terms by which the longitude prize could yet be won. This new act of 1774 repealed all the previous legislation on longitude. Its terms for trying new timekeepers threw up the strictest conditions yet: All entries must be submitted in duplicate, then undergo trials consisting of a full year's

OPPOSITE *King George III (1738-1820) succeeded to the throne of England in 1760. Like Charles II, he was interested in science and had an unusual appreciation for scientific instruments. This portrait was painted about the time that H-5 was tested in his private observatory.*

OPPOSITE *The award to Harrison of the £8,750 balance of the prize money did not please certain members of Parliament or the Board of Longitude, who determined that they would not allow themselves to be outmaneuvered again. Although the longitude problem had been solved, the solution needed considerable refinement to bring it into regular use. Therefore in 1774, Parliament passed this new act, which repealed all previous acts relating to finding longitude at sea and offered a maximum reward of £10,000 for finding longitude to within half a degree. The stipulations for the trial were so stringent, however, that the prize was never won.*

testing at Greenwich followed by two voyages around Great Britain (one heading east first, the other west), as well as any other voyages to whatever destinations the board might specify, culminating in up to twelve additional months of postvoyage observation at the Royal Observatory. Maskelyne was heard chortling that the act "had given the mechanics a bone to pick that would crack their teeth."

These words proved prophetic, for the prize money was never claimed.

Harrison, however, felt further vindicated in July 1775, when Cook returned from his second voyage with bouquets of praise for the method of finding longitude by means of a timekeeper.

"Mr Kendall's Watch (which cost £450)," the captain reported, "exceeded the expectations of its most zealous advocate and by being now and then corrected by lunar observations has been our faithful guide through all vicissitudes of climates."

RIGHT *The king's private observatory in Richmond Park (now known as Kew Observatory) was constructed for the 1769 transit of Venus, which the king wished to observe. Equipped with the most up-to-date astronomical instruments by the finest instrument makers, it was as suitable as the Royal Observatory for testing the going of H-5.*

The log of H.M.S. *Resolution* reveals numerous references to the timekeeper, which Cook called "our trusty friend the Watch," and "our never failing guide, the Watch." With its help, he made the first—and highly accurate—charts of the South Sea Islands.

"It would not be doing justice to Mr Harrison and Mr Kendall," Cook also noted in the log, "if I did not own that we have received very great assistance from this useful and valuable timepiece."

So enamored was Cook of K-1 that he carried it out on his third expedition, on July 12, 1776. This voyage was not so fortunate as the first two. Despite the great diplomacy of this renowned explorer, and his efforts to respect the native peoples of the lands he visited, Captain Cook ran into serious trouble in the Hawaiian archipelago.

At their initial encounter with Cook, who was the first white man they had ever seen, the Hawaiians hailed him as the incarnation of their god, Lono. But when he returned to their island some months later from his sorties around Alaska, tensions mounted, and Cook had to make a speedy departure. Within days, unfortunately, damage to the *Resolution*'s foremast forced him back to Kealakekua Bay. In the ensuing hostilities, Cook was murdered.

Almost at the instant the captain died in 1779, according to an account kept at the time, K-1 also stopped ticking.

( 1487 )

ANNO DECIMO QUARTO

# Georgii III. Regis.

C A P. LXVI.

An Act for the Repeal of all former Acts concerning the Longitude at Sea, except so much thereof as relates to the Appointment and Authority of the Commissioners thereby constituted, and also such Clauses as relate to the constructing, printing, publishing, vending, and licensing, of Nautical Almanacks, and other useful Tables; and for the more effectual Encouragement and Reward of such Person and Persons as shall discover a Method for finding the same, or shall make useful Discoveries in Navigation; and for the better making Experiments relating thereto.

WHEREAS an Act was made in the Twelfth Year of the Reign of Her late Majesty Queen Anne, intituled, An Act for providing a publick Reward for such Person or Persons as shall discover the Longitude at Sea; and also another Act was made in the fourteenth Year of the Reign of this late Majesty King George the Second, intituled, An Act for surveying the Chief Ports and Headlands on the Coasts

Preamble.

Act 12 Ann.

Act 14 Geo. II.

17 D 2

of

8

## CHAPTER FOURTEEN

# The Mass Production of Genius

The stars are not wanted now; put out every one,
Pack up the moon and dismantle the sun.

W. H. AUDEN, "Song"

WHEN JOHN HARRISON DIED, on March 24, 1776, exactly eighty-three years to the day after his birth in 1693, he held martyr status among clockmakers.

For decades he had stood apart, virtually alone, as the only person in the world seriously pursuing a timekeeper solution to the longitude problem. Then suddenly, in the wake of Harrison's success with H-4, legions of watchmakers took up the special calling of marine timekeeping. It became a boom industry in a maritime nation. Indeed, some modern horologists claim that Harrison's work facilitated England's mastery over the oceans, and thereby led to the creation of the British Empire—for it was by dint of the chronometer that Britannia ruled the waves.

In Paris, the great clockmakers Pierre Le Roy and Ferdinand Berthoud advanced their *montres marines* and *horloges marines* to perfection, but neither of these two archrivals ever produced a timekeeper design that could be reproduced quickly and cheaply.

Harrison's Watch, as the Board of Longitude never tired of reminding him, was too complex for ready reproduction, and awfully expensive, too. When Larcum Kendall copied it, the commissioners paid him a fee of £500 for his two-plus years of effort.

*Thomas Mudge's first marine timekeeper, shown here, was completed in 1774. It stopped during its first trial at Greenwich later in the same year, apparently due to mishandling by one of Maskelyne's assistants. On a second trial three years later, Maskelyne reported in the Board of Longitude minutes that it had gained only one minute, nineteen seconds in 109 days and was "greatly superior to any timekeeper which hath come under his inspection." Its performance after this, however, did not remain constant.*

# PIERRE LE ROY AND FERDINAND BERTHOUD

Pierre Le Roy was the eldest son of Julien Le Roy, the most celebrated clockmaker in France during the first half of the eighteenth century. His first marine timekeeper, which ran for only six hours, was completed in 1756. Seven years later, he presented a second machine, three feet high, to the Académie Royale des Sciences, but neither machine was ever tested on a voyage. On August 5, 1766, he presented to the king his "montre A," shown here, which was tried at sea between May and August 1767, along with an almost identical timekeeper, "montre S." These were the first timekeepers to incorporate three

of the essential elements of what became known as the marine chronometer: a detached chronometer escapement, an isochronal balance spring, and temperature compensation mounted in the balance itself. Le Roy's remarkable contributions were never properly recognized at the time, however, because of a young and highly ambitious rival, Ferdinand Berthoud *(left)*.

Ferdinand Berthoud (1727-1807), one of the most prolific clockmakers and horological writers of all time, was born in Switzerland and became a master watchmaker in France when he was twenty-six. In 1763 and 1766, he was sent on official visits to London to discover the secrets of Harrison's H-4 but did not learn enough to take the invention back to France. Berthoud's work is characterized by a large number of different designs (he produced about seventy marine timekeepers). Although his work was at the forefront of the development of the marine chronometer, none of his machines can be singled out as providing any fundamental advance.

In 1770, Berthoud was appointed "Horloger Mécanicien du Roi et de la Marine" and granted an annual pension of 3,000 livres. This illustration, from his *Traité des Horloges Marines* of 1773, was evidently intended to convince King Louis XV, to whom the book was dedicated, that the author's work represented future peace and progress for France: France's shipping interests would at last be safe; not even Athena, the goddess of war, would have anything to do but rest, knowing that Louis XV no longer needed her help. Berthoud's flattery paid off: His pension was immediately increased to 4,500 livres.

Asked to train other watchmakers to make more copies, Kendall backed off, on the grounds that the product was way too pricey.

"I am of the opinion," Kendall told the board, "that it would be many years (if ever) before a watch of the same kind with that of Mr. Harrison's could be afforded for £200."

Meanwhile, a seaman could buy a good sextant and a set of lunar distance tables for only a fraction of that sum, about £20. With such a glaring cost comparison between the two methods, the marine timekeeper had to provide more than ease of use and greater accuracy. It had to become more affordable.

Kendall tried to topple Harrison with a cheap imitation of the original Watch. Having produced K-1 in H-4's image, Kendall completed K-2 in 1772 after a second two-year period of devotion. He was paid £200 for it by the Board of Longitude. Although K-2 was

LEFT *This watch, Larcum Kendall's second marine timekeeper (K-2), was used by Captain Bligh on his infamous voyage aboard the* Bounty *in 1789. When the mutiny took place and Bligh was set adrift with eighteen others in a small boat, K-2 remained with the mutineers on Pitcairn Island. In 1808, it was purchased by the captain of an American whaler and taken to Chile, where it was later sold in Valparaiso for fifty guineas to a captain who took it back to England in 1843.*

RIGHT *The backplate of K-2 shows the spiral brass and steel compensation curb. K-2, like its predecessors K-1 and H-4, was not mounted in gimbals, and so the watch, while being secured inside its box on the ship, was subjected to the motion of the vessel. Kendall recognized that a sudden, sharp tilting was liable to move the straight bimetallic compensation curb under its own weight and thereby affect the timekeeper's performance. He overcame this problem by forming the compensation curb into a spiral, known from its appearance as a "Chelsea bun."*

about the size of K-1 and H-4, it was internally inferior, because Kendall had omitted the remontoire, the mechanism that doles out the power from the mainspring so the force applied to the timekeeping element stays the same whether the watch has just been wound up or is nearly wound down. Absent the remontoire, the timepiece ran fast at first, after winding, and then slowed down. The H-4 remontoire had been hailed by all who knew enough to appreciate it. Without it, K-2 proved undistinguished during tests at Greenwich.

The sea life of K-2, however, encompasses some of the most famous voyages in the annals of the oceans. The timepiece ventured out with a North Polar expedition, spent several years in North America, sailed to Africa, and boarded H.M.S. *Bounty* under Captain William Bligh. The captain's foul temper provides the stuff of legend, but an

*The mutiny on the* Bounty *took place on April 28, 1789. The captain's cabin, where K-2 would have been kept, was located at the stern of the ship, seen here occupied by the mutineers.*

unsung part of his story holds that when the mutiny on the *Bounty* occurred, in 1789, the crew made off with K-2. They kept the watch at Pitcairn Island until 1808, when the captain of an American whaling ship bought it and launched K-2 on yet another round of adventures.

In 1774 Kendall made a third, still cheaper timekeeper (minus the diamonds this time), which he sold to the board for £100. K-3 performed no better than K-2, yet it shipped passage on H.M.S. *Discovery* to take part in Cook's third tour. (Bligh, incidentally, served as sailing master under Captain Cook on this voyage. And although Cook was killed in Hawaii, Bligh went on to become governor of New South Wales, Australia, where he was imprisoned by army mutineers during the Rum Rebellion.)

None of Kendall's own innovations compared with his masterful copy work on K-1. He soon ceased trying new ideas, already outstripped by others far more inventive than he.

One of these was watchmaker Thomas Mudge of Fleet Street, who had been apprenticed in his youth to "Honest" George Graham. Like Kendall, Mudge attended the dissection and discussion of H-4 at Harrison's house. Later he indiscreetly divulged those details at dinner with Ferdinand Berthoud, though he swore he intended no wrongdoing. Mudge had an earned reputation as a fine craftsman and a fair tradesman. He constructed his first marine timekeeper in 1774, incorporating and improving upon many of Harrison's ideas. Enviably executed inside and out, the Mudge chronometer boasted a special form of remontoire and an eight-sided gilt case crowned by a face full of silver filigree. He later made another two in 1777, called "Green" and "Blue"—a matched pair, identical except for the colors of their cases—to compete in earnest for the remaining £10,000 of the longitude prize.

While testing Mudge's first timekeeper at Greenwich, Astronomer Royal Nevil Maskelyne unwittingly made it stop running through mishandling, and within another month accidentally *broke* the device's mainspring. The much-disgruntled Mudge then took Harrison's place as Maskelyne's new sparring partner. The two kept up a lively exchange of opinions until Mudge became ill in the early 1790s. At that point, Mudge's lawyer son, Thomas Jr., carried on the dispute, some of it in pamphlet form, and won a £3,000 payment from the Board of Longitude in recognition of his father's contributions.

While Kendall and Mudge each built three marine timekeepers apiece in the course of a lifetime, and Harrison five, the watchmaker John Arnold finished several hundred of high quality. His prodigious output may have been even greater than we know, since Arnold, a canny marketer, often engraved "No. 1" on a watch that was by no means the first of its kind in a particular product line. The secret to Arnold's speedy manufacture lay in the way he farmed out the bulk of the routine work to various craftsmen and did only the difficult parts, especially the meticulous adjusting, himself.

As Arnold's star rose, the word *chronometer* came into general usage as the preferred name for a marine timekeeper. Jeremy Thacker had coined this term in 1714, but it didn't catch on until 1779, when it appeared in the title of a pamphlet by Alexander Dalrymple of the East India Company, *Some Notes Useful to Those Who Have Chronometers at Sea.*

"The machine used for measuring time at sea is here named chronometer," Dalrymple explained, "[as] so valuable a machine deserves to be known by a name instead of a definition."

Arnold's first three box chronometers, which he supplied to the Board of Longitude, traveled, as did K-1, with Captain Cook. The whole Arnold trio sailed on the 1772-75 voyage to the Antarctic and the South Pacific. The "vicissitudes of cli-

OPPOSITE *After his seven-year apprenticeship to George Graham, Thomas Mudge (1715-94) established an excellent reputation as a maker of complicated watches. About 1754, he invented the detached lever escapement, the most common form of escapement used in mechanical watches even today. Mudge was one of the three watchmakers chosen to examine H-4 when Harrison disclosed the secrets of its mechanism on August 14, 1765. A few years later, due to ill health, Mudge moved from London to Plymouth, where he produced his first marine timekeeper in 1774. The new Longitude Act, passed in the same year, required each applicant to submit not one but two timekeepers in order to qualify for the £10,000 prize. Aided by an advance of £500, within three years Mudge produced two identical timekeepers, known as "Blue" and "Green" from the color of their cases. Although these exquisite timepieces underwent three trials at Greenwich, their performance under Maskelyne's watchful eye did not qualify them for a reward. Mudge's son, however, was a lawyer, and, after much petitioning, he won a further £2,500 for his father in 1793.*

*John Arnold (1735-99) was a prolific maker who contributed much toward the design and manufacture of the standard marine timekeeper. Unlike Harrison, Kendall, Mudge, and Le Roy, who took a year or more to make one machine, Arnold produced more than 1,000 timekeepers during his lifetime and, in doing so, devised ways of greatly reducing the cost of production. His interest in marine timekeeping was influenced by* The Principles of Mr. Harrison's Timekeeper, *which Nevil Maskelyne gave him in 1767. This publication inspired him to produce his first marine timekeeper in the following year, and, in 1771, two of his machines were tested successfully at sea. When Cook departed on his second voyage in 1772, three of the four timekeepers taken were made by Arnold, but none of his performed reliably. Arnold persevered, however, developing the pivoted detent escapement in 1774 and patenting the helical balance spring and a temperature-compensated balance in 1775. Success came in 1779, when his famous watch, No. 36, performed with unprecedented accuracy during its trial at Greenwich.*

186

mates," as Cook described the global weather range, caused Arnold's clocks to go poorly. Cook declared himself unimpressed with the way they performed aboard his two ships.

The board cut off Arnold's funding as a result. But this action, instead of discouraging the young watchmaker, spurred him on to new concepts, all of which he patented and perpetually improved. In 1779 he created a sensation with a pocket chronometer, called No. 36. It truly was small enough to be worn in the pocket, and Maskelyne and his deputies carried it in theirs for thirteen months to test its accuracy. From one day to the next, it never gained or lost more than three seconds.

Meanwhile, Arnold continued to hone his skill at mass production. He opened a factory at Well Hall, south London, in 1785. His competitor, Thomas Mudge Jr., tried to run a factory, too, turning out some thirty imitations of his father's chronometers. But Thomas Jr. was a lawyer, not a clockmaker. No timekeeper that came from the junior Mudge works ever matched the accuracy of the elder's three originals. And yet, a Mudge chronometer cost twice as much as one of Arnold's.

Arnold did everything methodically. He established his reputation in his early twenties by making a marvelous miniature watch, only half an inch in diameter, which he mounted in a finger ring and presented to King George III as a gift in 1764. Arnold married *after* he had laid out his lifework as a maker of marine timekeepers. He chose a wife who was not only well-to-do but also well prepared to improve his business as well as his home life. Together they invested their all in their only child, John Roger Arnold, who also tried to further the family enterprise. John Roger studied watchmaking in Paris under the finest teachers of his father's choosing, and when he became full partner in 1784, the company name changed to Arnold and Son. But Arnold Sr. always remained the better watchmaker of the two. His brain bubbled over with myriad ways to do things, and he seems to have tried them all in his chronometers. Most of his best mousetraps were artful simplifications of things Harrison had pioneered in a clever but complicated way.

The octagonal-shaped case of this chronometer, No. 32/122, made by John Arnold and Son in 1792, was typical of the outward appearance of Arnold's marine chronometers during this period. This all-wood design, however, did not provide an adequate seal for the movement. In addition to the problems of moisture rusting the steel parts, there was more than one instance of a spider finding its way through the winding hole into the timekeeper, with unfortunate consequences for both. It was not until 1795 or later that the movements of his chronometers were fitted into a more protective brass bowl.

188

*The movement of John Arnold and Son chronometer No. 32/122 is fitted with a gold helical balance spring and Arnold's "YZ" nonferrous bimetallic balance. Arnold used these materials to overcome the problems of rust and magnetism.*

Arnold's biggest competition came from Thomas Earnshaw, who ushered in the age of the truly modern chronometer. Earnshaw reduced Harrison's complexity and Arnold's prolificacy to an almost platonic essence of chronometer. Equally important, he brought one of Harrison's biggest ideas down to small scale at last, by devising a timekeeping element that needed no oil.

Earnshaw lacked Arnold's finesse and business sense. He married a poor woman, fathered too many children, and mismanaged his financial affairs so badly that he had to serve time in debtors' prison. Nevertheless, it was Earnshaw who changed the chronometer from a special-order curiosity into an assembly-line item. His own economic need may have inspired him in this pursuit: By sticking to a single basic design

*189*

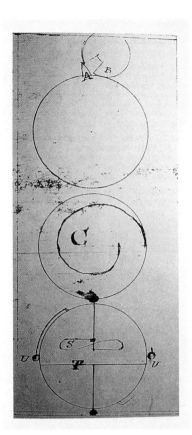

*The drawing for Arnold's spring detent escapement (No. 1328, filed in 1782, top drawing ), is so incomplete that it is surprising a patent was granted.*

OPPOSITE *Earnshaw reluctantly agreed that the patent for his spring detent escapement (No. 1354, filed in 1783), the drawing for which is shown at the bottom, would be listed in the name of watchmaker Thomas Wright, who paid the one-hundred-guinea fee that Earnshaw could not afford.*

(unlike Arnold, who was almost too inventive for his own good), Earnshaw could turn out an Earnshaw chronometer in about two months and then turn the chronometer into ready cash.

In addition to being commercial competitors, Arnold and Earnshaw became sworn enemies in a fight over their conflicting originality claims for the chronometer's key component, called the spring detent escapement. An escapement lies at the core of any watch or clock; it alternately blocks and releases the movement at a rhythm set by the clock's regulator. Chronometers, which aspire to perfect timekeeping, are defined by the design of their escapement. Harrison had used his grasshopper escapement in the big sea clocks, then turned to a brilliant modification of the old-fashioned verge escapement in H-4. Mudge won lasting acclaim for his lever escapement, which appeared in nearly all mechanical wrist- and pocket watches manufactured through the middle of the twentieth century, including the famous Ingersoll dollar watch, the original Mickey Mouse watch, and the early Timex watches. Arnold appeared entirely happy with his pivoted detent escapement—until he heard about Earnshaw's spring detent escapement in 1782. It was an "Aha!" moment for Arnold, who realized right away that replacing pivots with a spring would eliminate any need to oil that part of the works.

Arnold couldn't get a look at Earnshaw's escapement, but he contrived his own version, then rushed to the patent office with sketches. Earnshaw, who lacked the money to patent his invention, nevertheless had proof of paternity in watches he'd made for others—and in the joint-patent bargain he had arranged with established watchmaker Thomas Wright.

The fracas between Arnold and Earnshaw polarized the whole community of London watchmakers, not to mention the Royal Society and the Board of Longitude. Great quantities of ink and bile were expended by both parties and their various supporters. Enough evidence emerged to prove that Arnold had peeked inside one of Earnshaw's watches before he filed his patent, but who was to say he hadn't been thinking of such a mechanism on his own? Arnold and Earnshaw never settled their differences to either one's satisfaction. Indeed, the brouhaha lives on today among historians who continue to find new evidence and take sides in the old argument.

The Board of Longitude, egged on by Maskelyne, in 1803 declared Earnshaw's chronometers to run better than any previously tried at the Royal Observatory. Maskelyne had at last met a watchmaker he liked, though it is not clear *why* he liked him. Whatever the reason, Earnshaw's fine craftsmanship provoked the astronomer royal to proffer advice, encouragement, and opportunities for clock repair work at the Observatory—a pattern of patronage that persisted for more than a decade. Earnshaw, however, who described himself as "irritable by nature," gave Maskelyne the hard time he had no doubt come to expect from "mechanics." For example, Earnshaw attacked Maskelyne's yearlong trials for testing chronometers, and succeeded in getting these shortened to six months.

In 1805, the Board of Longitude awarded Thomas Earnshaw and John Roger Arnold (Arnold Sr. having died in 1799) equal awards of £3,000 each—the same amount that had gone to Mayer's and Mudge's heirs. Earnshaw shouted and published his indignation, for he thought he deserved a larger share. Fortunately for Earnshaw, he was making a comfortable living by then from his commercial success.

A.D. 1783. FEBR. 1. Nº 1354.
WRIGHT'S SPECIFICATION.

*The enrolled drawing is not colored.*

*Thomas Earnshaw (1749-1829) perfected the design of the marine chronometer and developed the methods by which it could be produced in quantity at a reasonable cost. Earnshaw had a large family, and it was not until the 1790s that he was able to pay his debts and establish his own business. Despite several attempts, he was unable to win the 1774 £10,000 longitude prize, but, with the support of Astronomer Royal Nevil Maskelyne, the Board of Longitude recognized his contributions in 1805 by awarding him £3,000. Earnshaw, however, was bitterly dissatisfied with this sum when he learned that the same amount had been granted posthumously to his arch-rival, John Arnold.*

Captains of the East India Company and the Royal Navy flocked to the chronometer factories. At the peak of the Arnold-Earnshaw contretemps in the 1780s, prices had come down to about £80 for an Arnold box chronometer and £65 for an Earnshaw. Pocket chronometers could be bought for even less. Although naval officers had to pay for a chronometer out of their own pockets, most were pleased to make the purchase. Logbooks of the 1780s bear this out, for they begin to show daily references to longitude readings by timekeeper. In 1791, the East India Company issued new logbooks to the captains of its commercial vessels, with preprinted pages that contained a special column for "longitude by Chronometer." Many navy captains continued to rely on lunars, when the skies allowed them to, but the chronometer's credibility grew and grew. In comparison tests, chronometers proved themselves an order of magnitude more precise than lunars, primarily because they were simpler to use. The unwieldy lunar method, which demanded a series of astronomical observations, ephemerides consultations, and corrective computations, opened many doors through which error could enter.

By the turn of the century, the navy had procured a stock of chronometers for storage in Portsmouth, at the Naval Academy, where a captain could claim one as he prepared to sail from that port. With supply small and demand high, however, officers frequently found the academy's cupboard bare and continued to buy their own.

Arnold, Earnshaw, and an increasing number of contemporaries sold chronometers at home and abroad for use on naval ships, merchant vessels, and even pleasure yachts. Thus the total world census of marine timekeepers grew from just one in 1737 to approximately five thousand instruments by 1815.

When the Board of Longitude disbanded in 1828, at the repeal of the prevailing Longitude Act, its chief duty, ironically enough, had become the supervision of testing and assigning chronometers to ships of the Royal Navy. In 1829, the navy's own hydrographer (chief chartmaker) took over the responsibility. This was a big job, as it included seeing to the rate setting of new machines and the repair of old ones, as well as the delicate transportation of the chronometers over land, from factory to seaport and back again.

It was not uncommon for one ship to rely on two or even three chronometers, so that the several timekeepers could keep tabs on each other. Big surveying ships might carry as many as forty chronometers. Records show that when H.M.S. *Beagle* set out

LEFT *This unsigned spring detent escapement watch, hallmarked 1784, is one of the first watches made by Earnshaw as part of his agreement with Wright to repay the cost of the patent. Earnshaw would make and sell the watches for the price he wanted, but the retailing watchmaker would be obliged to pay Wright one guinea for the mark "Wright's Patent" stamped on each watch sold. This mark and the fee would be continued until the cost of the patent had been satisfied. These watches, whether sold by Wright or another watchmaker, were engraved only with the name of the retailer, not the maker—a common practice at the time.*

RIGHT *The movement of this watch was made by Earnshaw for Wright, but signed by Wright. This may be one of the first twelve watches that Earnshaw stated he made for Wright. The original design of the escapement caused these watches to stop on occasion, and Earnshaw claimed that he had to remake the escapements of all of them at his own expense. The spring detent in this watch, unlike later versions of the escapement, has only a single spring for locking and unlocking, as shown in the patent drawing.*

*Marine chronometer No. 928 made by Earnshaw, c. 1812, was typical of the design he had perfected by 1790. It was generally priced at sixty-five guineas. Arnold's marine chronometers were priced from sixty to eighty guineas.*

OPPOSITE LEFT *This standard marine chronometer was purchased by the Admiralty in 1841 and used aboard the* Wilberforce *on its surveying expedition up the River Niger in 1841 and 1842. Its records show that the chronometer was engaged in continuous service on several different vessels (on the Australian survey between 1887 and 1889 and throughout World War I) until 1922, a period of more than eighty years. This record of performance, with only routine maintenance, was not uncommon for a chronometer and gives an insight into how well these timekeepers were designed and made.*

194

in 1831, bent on fixing the longitudes of foreign lands, she had twenty-two chronometers along to do the job. Half of these had been supplied by the Admiralty, while six belonged personally to Captain Robert Fitzroy, who had the remaining five on loan. This same long voyage of the *Beagle* introduced its official naturalist, the young Charles Darwin, to the wildlife of the Galápagos Islands.

In 1860, when the Royal Navy counted fewer than two hundred ships on all seven seas, it owned close to eight hundred chronometers. Clearly, this was an idea whose time had come. The infinite practicality of John Harrison's approach had been demonstrated so thoroughly that its once formidable competition simply disappeared. Having established itself securely on shipboard, the chronometer was soon taken for granted, like any other essential thing, and the whole question of its contentious history, along with the name of its original inventor, dropped from the consciousness of the seamen who used it every day.

ABOVE RIGHT *By 1790, the marine chronometer's fundamental design was so refined that it remained virtually unaltered until the development of quartz crystal changed the principles upon which the mechanism worked. The design became associated with accuracy and reliability: this timekeeper, made by A. Lange & Söhne in Germany in 1944, when both materials and skilled labor were extremely scarce, maintains the outward appearance of a marine chronometer, but its movement is only that of a high-quality pocket watch.*

## CHAPTER FIFTEEN

# In the Meridian Courtyard

"What's the good of Mercator's North Poles and Equators,
  Tropics, Zones, and Meridian Lines?"
So the Bellman would cry: and the crew would reply
  "They are merely conventional signs!"

LEWIS CARROLL, "The Hunting of the Snark"

I AM STANDING on the prime meridian of the world, zero degrees longitude, the center of time and space, literally the place where East meets West. It's paved right into the courtyard of the Old Royal Observatory at Greenwich. At night, buried lights shine through the glass-covered meridian line, so it glows like a man-made midocean rift, splitting the globe in two equal halves with all the authority of the Equator. For a little added fanfare after dark, a green laser projects the meridian's visibility ten miles across the valley to Essex.

Unstoppable as a comic book superhero, the line cuts through the nearby structures. It appears as a brass strip on the wooden floors of the Meridian House, then transforms into a single row of red blips that recall an airplane's emergency exit lighting system. Outside, where the prime meridian threads its way among the cobblestones, concrete slab stripes run alongside it, with brass letters and tick marks announcing the names and longitudes of the world's great cities.

A strategically placed machine offers to issue me a souvenir ticket stamped with the precise moment—to one-hundredth of a second—when I straddled the prime merid-

*This modern view of the prime meridian of the world looks toward the building housing the transit circle, the instrument upon which Greenwich Mean Time was based. The old brass strip marking the line of the meridian across the courtyard has been replaced by fiber optic lights. Although the Royal Observatory left this historic location at Greenwich shortly before World War II, the Greenwich meridian still remains the point of zero longitude, the reference for determining Coordinated Universal Time. This meridian was established by the Astronomer Royal George Airy in 1851 (nineteen feet east of the meridian used since 1750) and was adopted as the prime meridian of the world in 1884.*

*These views of the Greenwich Observatory appeared in 1885, the year after it was adopted as the prime meridian of the world. The prime meridian runs through the center of Airy's transit circle telescope (far left), which was installed in 1850 for determining the precise time. Observations with this instrument commenced on January 4, 1851. By observing the exact moment that a star crossed the meridian, the observatory clocks could be maintained to a high degree of accuracy for the distribution of Greenwich time.*

ian. But this is just a sideshow attraction, with a price of £1 per ticket. Actual Greenwich mean time, by which the world sets its watch, is indicated far more precisely, to within millionths of seconds, inside the Meridian House on an atomic clock whose digital display changes too fast for the eye to follow.

Nevil Maskelyne, fifth astronomer royal, brought the prime meridian to this location, seven miles from the heart of London. During the years he lived on the Observatory site, from 1765 to his death in 1811, Maskelyne published forty-nine issues of the comprehensive *Nautical Almanac.* He figured all of the lunar-solar and lunar-stellar distances listed in the *Almanac* from the Greenwich meridian. And so, starting with the very first volume in 1767, sailors all over the world who relied on Maskelyne's tables began to calculate their longitude from Greenwich. Previously, they had been content to express their position as degrees east or west of any convenient meridian. Most often they used their point of departure—"three degrees twenty-seven minutes west of the Lizard," for example— or their destination. But Maskelyne's tables not only made the lunar distance method practicable, they also made the Greenwich meridian the universal reference point. Even the French translations of the *Nautical Almanac* retained Maskelyne's calculations from Greenwich—in spite of the fact that every other table in the *Connaissance des Temps* considered the Paris meridian as the prime.

This homage to Greenwich might have been expected to diminish after chronometers triumphed over lunars as the method of choice for finding longitude. But in fact the opposite occurred. Navigators still needed to make lunar distance observations from time to time, in order to verify their chronometers. Opening to the appropriate pages in

*In 1833, the Royal Observatory at Greenwich provided one of the first visual time signals by installing a time ball on the eastern turret. The instant that the ball was dropped (at 1 P.M. each day) allowed navigators aboard their ships in the adjacent reaches of the River Thames to regulate and rate their chronometers precisely. One o'clock was chosen because at noon astronomers were often occupied with observations of the meridian transit of the sun.*

the *Nautical Almanac,* they naturally computed their longitude east or west of Greenwich, no matter where they had come from or where they were going. Cartographers who sailed on mapping voyages to uncharted lands likewise recorded the longitudes of those places with respect to the Greenwich meridian.

In 1884, at the International Meridian Conference held in Washington, D.C., representatives from twenty-six countries voted to make the common practice official. They declared the Greenwich meridian the prime meridian of the world. This decision did not sit well with the French, however, who continued to recognize their own Paris Observatory meridian, a little more than two degrees east of Greenwich, as the starting line for another twenty-seven years, until 1911. (Even then, they hesitated to refer directly to Greenwich mean time, preferring the locution "Paris Mean Time, retarded by nine minutes twenty-one seconds.")

The gate clock at the old main entrance to the Royal Observatory was the first clock to make Greenwich time available to the public. The master clock, which was installed in the Observatory in 1852, controlled the hands of this clock, the dropping of the time ball, and the distribution of time signals via telegraph lines to the railways.

Since time is longitude and longitude time, the Old Royal Observatory is also the keeper of the stroke of midnight. Day begins at Greenwich. Time zones the world over run a legislated number of hours ahead of or behind Greenwich mean time (GMT). Greenwich time even extends into outer space: Astronomers use GMT to time predictions and observations, except that they call it Universal Time, or UT, in their celestial calendars.

*The most precise method available at present to determine the coordinates of a location is by satellite navigation, known as GPS (Global Positioning System). Signals must be received from three satellites to find latitude and longitude on Earth.*

Half a century before the entire world population began taking its time cues from Greenwich, the observatory officials provided a visual signal from the top of Flamsteed House to ships in the Thames. When naval captains were anchored on the river, they could set their chronometers by the dropping of a ball every day at thirteen hundred hours—1 P.M.

Though modern ships rely on radio and satellite signals, the ceremony of the ball continues on a daily basis in the Meridian Courtyard, as it has done every day since 1833. People expect it, like teatime. Accordingly, at 12:55 P.M., a slightly battered red ball climbs halfway up the mast to the weather vane. It hovers there for three minutes, by way of warning. Then it ascends to its summit and waits another two minutes. Mobs of school groups and self-conscious adults find themselves craning their necks, staring at this target, which resembles nothing so much as an antiquated diving bell.

This more frequent, oddly anachronistic event has a genteel feel. How lovely the red metal looks against the blue October sky, where a stout west wind drives puffs of clouds over the twin observatory towers. Even the youngest children are quiet, expectant.

At one o'clock, the ball drops, like a fireman descending a very short pole. Nothing about the motion even suggests high technology or precision timekeeping. Yet it was this ball and other time balls and time guns at ports around the world that finally gave mariners a way to reckon their chronometers—without resorting to lunars more than once every few weeks at sea.

*Time signals transmitted from satellites are measured against atomic frequency standards in different parts of the world. The U.S. Naval Observatory Alternate Master Clock at Falcon Air Force Base in Colorado, shown here, serves one of the five stations that monitor the GPS time signals and does not vary from the time of the master clock in Washington, D.C., by more than three nanoseconds (0.000,000,003 second, or the time it takes light to travel three feet). With this timing precision, a military handheld GPS receiver can pinpoint a location to within sixteen meters. For security reasons, in commercial receivers the signals are encoded to limit their instantaneous position accuracy to about one hundred meters.*

Inside Flamsteed House, where Harrison first sought the advice and counsel of Edmond Halley in 1730, the Harrison timekeepers hold court in their present places of honor. The big sea clocks, H-1, H-2, and H-3, were brought here to Greenwich in a rather dishonorable fashion, after being rudely removed from Harrison's house on May 23, 1766. Maskelyne never wound them, nor tended to them after testing them, but simply consigned them to a damp storage area where they were forgotten for the rest of his lifetime—and where they remained for another twenty-five years following his death. By the time one of John Roger Arnold's associates, E.J. Dent, offered to clean the big clocks for free in 1836, the necessary refurbishing required a four-year effort on Dent's part. Some of the blame for the sea clocks' deterioration lay with their original cases, which were not airtight. However, Dent put the cleaned timekeepers back in their cases just as he'd found them, inviting a new round of decay to commence immediately.

When Lieutenant Commander Rupert T. Gould of the Royal Navy took an interest in the timekeepers in 1920, he later recalled, "All were dirty, defective and corroded—

*Lieutenant Commander Rupert T. Gould (1890-1948) is shown here with H-2, c. 1930. His painstaking work over a period of thirteen years and the descriptions of the timekeepers in his publications established the importance of these machines and ensured their future preservation. When Gould discovered H-1 around 1920, many parts were missing and all those made of steel had to be replaced. The rebuilding of this timekeeper began in 1931, and on February 1, 1933, it was running once again. In 1931, it underwent further restoration.*

while No. 1, in particular, looked as though it had gone down with the *Royal George* and had been on the bottom ever since. It was completely covered—even the wooden portions—with a bluish-green patina."

Gould, a man of great sensitivity, was so appalled by this pitiful neglect that he sought permission to restore all four (the three clocks and the Watch) to working order. He offered to do the work, which took him twelve years, without pay, and despite the fact that he had no horological training.

"I reflected that, so far as that was concerned, Harrison and I were in the same boat," Gould remarked with typical good humor, "and that if I started with No. 1 I could scarcely do that machine any further harm." So he set to right away with an ordinary hat brush, removing two full ounces of dirt and verdigris from H-1.

Tragic events in Gould's own life inured him to the difficulty of the job he had volunteered for. Compared to the mental breakdown he suffered at the outset of World War I, which barred him from active duty, and his unhappy marriage and separation, described in the *Daily Mail* in such lurid detail that he lost his naval commission, the years of attic seclusion with the strange, obsolete timepieces were positively therapeutic for Gould. By putting them to rights, he nursed himself back to health and peace of mind.

*These four views, taken about 1920, are the only known photographs of H-1 before it was restored by Gould. H-1 had been badly damaged during transit from Harrison's house to the Royal Observatory on May 23, 1766. By 1840, it was in a complete state of decay.*

ABOVE LEFT *Of Harrison's three sea clocks, H-2, shown here around 1920, before restoration, was in the best condition. Since its arrival in the Observatory, it had been cleaned only once, in 1840. In 1923, Gould devoted a year to its restoration.*

ABOVE RIGHT *H-3, also shown around 1920, before restoration, took Harrison nineteen years to complete and Gould seven years to restore.*

It seems only proper that more than half of Gould's repair work—seven years by his count—fell to H-3, which had taken Harrison the longest time to build. Indeed, Harrison's problems begat Gould's:

"No. 3 is not merely complicated, like No. 2," Gould told a gathering of the Society for Nautical Research in 1935, "it is abstruse. It embodies several devices which are entirely unique—devices which no clockmaker has ever thought of using, and which Harrison invented as the result of tackling his mechanical problems as an engineer might, and not as a clockmaker would." In more than one instance, Gould found to his chagrin that "remains of some device which Harrison had tried and subsequently discarded had been left *in situ*." He had to pick through these red herrings to find the devices truly deserving of salvage.

Unlike Dent before him, who had merely cleaned the machines and sawed off the rough edges of broken pieces to make them look neat, Gould wanted to make everything whir and tick and keep perfect time again.

While he worked, Gould filled eighteen notebooks with meticulous colored-ink drawings and elaborate verbal descriptions far clearer than any Harrison ever wrote. These he intended for his own use, to guide him through repetitions of difficult procedures, and to save himself the needless repetition of costly mistakes. The removal or replacement of the escapements in H-3, for example, routinely took eight hours, and Gould was forced to go through the routine at least forty times.

As for H-4, the Watch, "It took me three days to learn the trick of getting the hands off," Gould reported. "I more than once believed that they were welded on."

*Although Gould states that he set H-1 going in 1933, it is evident from the date on this page from the notebook he kept during the restoration that he continued working with it during the next two years.*

Although he cleaned H-1 first, he restored it last. This turned out to be a good thing, since H-1 was missing so many pieces that Gould needed the experience of exploring the others before he could handle H-1 with confidence: "There were no mainsprings, no mainspring-barrels, no chains, no escapements, no balance-springs, no banking-springs, and no winding gear . . . Five out of the twenty-four anti-friction wheels had vanished. Many parts of the complicated gridiron compensation were missing, and most of the others defective. The seconds-hand was gone and the hour-hand cracked. As for the small parts—pins, screws, etc.—scarcely one in ten remained."

The symmetry of H-1, however, and Gould's own determination, allowed him to duplicate many absent parts from their surviving counterparts.

"The worst job was the last," he confessed, "adjusting the little steel check-pieces on the balance-springs; a process which I can only describe as like trying to thread a needle stuck into the tailboard of a motor-lorry which you are chasing on a bicycle. I finished this, with a gale lashing the rain on to the windows of my garret, about 4 P.M. on February 1st, 1933—and five minutes later No. 1 had begun to go again for the first time since June 17th, 1767: an interval of 165 years."

Thanks to Gould's efforts, the clock is still going now, in the observatory gallery. The restored timepieces constitute John Harrison's enduring memorial, just as St. Paul's Cathedral serves as monument to Christopher Wren. Although Harrison's actual remains are entombed some miles northwest of Greenwich, in the cemetery of St. John's Church, Hampstead, where his wife, the second Elizabeth, and his son, William, lie buried with him, his mind and heart are here.

The Maritime Museum curator who now cares for the sea clocks refers to them reverently as "the Harrisons," as though they were a family of people instead of things. He dons white gloves to unlock their exhibit boxes and wind them, early every morning, before the visitors arrive. Each lock admits two different keys that work in concert, as on a modern safe deposit box—and reminiscent of the shared-key safeguards that prevailed in the clock trials of the eighteenth century.

H-1 requires one deft, downward pull on its brass-link chain. H-2 and H-3 take a turn with a winding key. That keeps them going. H-4 hibernates, unmoving and untouchable, mated for life with K-1 in the see-through cave they share.

Coming face-to-face with these machines at last—after having read countless accounts of their construction and trial, after having seen every detail of their insides and outsides in still and moving pictures—reduced me to tears. I wandered among them for hours, until I became distracted by a little girl about six years old, with a tussle of blond curls and a big Band-Aid angled above her left eye. She was viewing an automatically repeating color animation of the H-1 mechanism, over and over, sometimes staring intently at it, sometimes laughing out loud. In her excitement, she could

*John Harrison died on March 24, 1776, and was buried in Hampstead Parish church, his name being listed in the burial register as "Thomas Harrison." After falling into a state of disrepair, his tomb was completely restored at the expense of The Worshipful Company of Clockmakers in 1879.*

The Harrison gallery in the
Old Royal Observatory was
opened to the public in 1993 on
the 300th anniversary of
Harrison's birth. Prior to this
special exhibition, the
Harrison timekeepers were
exhibited in the west wing of
the National Maritime
Museum.

hardly keep her hands off the small television screen, although her father, when he caught her at this, pulled them away. With his permission, I asked her what it was she liked so much about the film.

"I don't know," she answered. "I just like it."

I liked it, too.

I liked the way the rocking, interconnected components kept their steady beat, even as the cartoon clock tilted to climb up and then slide down the shaded waves. A visual synecdoche, this clock came to life not only as the true time but also as a ship at sea, sailing mile after nautical mile over the bounding time zones.

With his marine clocks, John Harrison tested the waters of space-time. He succeeded, against all odds, in using the fourth—temporal—dimension to link points on the three-dimensional globe. He wrested the world's whereabouts from the stars, and locked the secret in a pocket watch.

# Illustration sources and credits

WCC/Bridgeman- Courtesy of the Worshipful Company of Clockmakers, London/Bridgeman Art Library, London
Houghton - By permission of the Houghton Library, Harvard University
NMM - Courtesy of the National Maritime Museum, Greenwich, London
NPG - Courtesy of the National Portrait Gallery, London
RS - By permission of the President and Council of the Royal Society, London
TM - Courtesy of The Time Museum, Rockford, Illinois

**p.i** see credit for p.117; **p.ii** see credits for pp.56 and 150; **p.v** from top, see credits for pp.26, 74, 62, 92.

## Chapter One
**Frontispiece p.viii** Sculpture of Atlas at Rockefeller Center by Lee Lawrie, January 1937. Photograph courtesy of George Gibson. **p.2** Manuscript of Oronce Fine's *Le Sphère du Monde* (Paris, 1549). By permission of the Department of Printing and Graphic Arts. Houghton (Ms Typ 57, p.67r). **p.3** World map, from Claudius Ptolemy, *Cosmographia* (Ulm, 1482). By permission of the Department of Printing and Graphic Arts, Houghton (Typ Inc 2556). **p.4** World map, from Claudius Ptolemy, *Geographia* ([Argentinae (Strasbourg), 1513]). By permission of the Department of Printing and Graphic Arts, Houghton (Typ 520.13.715 PF). **p.4** "Tabula Terra Incognita," from Claudius Ptolemy, *Geographia* ([Argentinae (Strasbourg), 1513]. By permission of the Department of Printing and Graphic Arts. Houghton (Typ 520.13.715 PF). **p.5** Diagram illustrating the tilt of the Earth's axis in relation to its orbit around the sun, from George Adams, *Astronomical and Geographical Essays* (London, 1795), vol. IV, plate V, fig. 2. Houghton (Astro 8005.1.12). **p.6** Table showing the number of miles in a degree of longitude at every degree of latitude, from *Encyclopaedia Britannica* (Edinburgh, 1771), vol. 3, p.372. Houghton (Typ 520.13.715 PF). **p.6** Diagram showing lines of longitude divided into hours, from Oronce Fine, *Sphaera Mundi* (Paris, 1551), p.17v. Houghton (FC5.F494.533de). **p.8** Winds and currents of the North and South Atlantic. Illustration by Jeffrey L. Ward Graphic Design. **p.9** Significant voyages of exploration. Illustration by Jeffrey L. Ward Graphic Design. **pp.10-11** The wreck of the *Amsterdam* by Cornelis Claesz van Wieringen (c. 1580-1633), 1599(?). NMM (Palmer Collection, BHC0724). **p.12** Title page from *Teerste Deel Vande* (Leyden, 1586), the Latin translation of Lucas Janszoon Waghenaer's *Spieghel der Zeevaerdt*. Houghton (*85-793F). **p.13** Page of a log book, from Captain John Davis (Davys), *The Seamans Secrets* (London, 1643). Courtesy of the Bodleian Library, Oxford (SAVILE.L.10.[2]).

## Chapter Two
**p.14** Portrait of Sir Clowdisley Shovell (c. 1650-1707) by Michael Dahl, c. 1702., NMM (BHC3025). **p.16** Richard Mount and Thomas Page, "Chart of the English Channel," published in *The English Pilot, Part V, describing the Sea-Coasts, Capes, Head-Lands*, 2d ed. (London, 1720), printed by R. and W. Mount and T. Page. Courtesy of the Harvard Map Collection, Harvard University (MA 5440 720.1 PF*). **p.17** The wreck of the *Association*, 1707. NMM (1034). **p.18** Sketch by Léon A. Morel-Fatio (1810-71) showing the log and line in use, published in Eugène Pacini, *La Marine, Arsenaux, Navires, Équipages, Navigation, Atterages, et Combats* (Paris, 1844). Courtesy of the Musée de la Marine, Paris. **p.19** Navigator using a compass, from Marco Polo, *Le Livre des Merveilles*. This copy was produced about 1410-12 for the duc de Bourgogne, who offered it in January 1413 to his uncle, the duc de Berry. Courtesy of the Bibliothèque Nationale, Paris (Fr. Ms. 2810, f. 188r). **p.21** Portrait of George Anson (1697-1762) by Sir Joshua Reynolds (1723-92), c. 1745. NMM (BHC2517). **p.22** Map showing the *Centurion's* voyage around Cape Horn in 1741, from George Anson, *Voyage around the World* (London, 1748), p.94. Houghton (SA 877.40.2*). **p.24** The capture of the *Nuestra Señora de Cobadonga* by the *Centurion* by Samuel Scott. NMM (BHC0360).

## Chapter Three
**p.26** Portrait of Galileo Galilei (1564-1642), possibly by Filippo di Nicola Furini, c. 1612. The authors appreciate the assistance of Mario Biagoli in pointing out the reference to Furini. Courtesy of Schloss Ambras, Austria, by permission of Erich Lessing/Art Resource (S0015107). **p.29** Illustration showing use of the cross-staff, from Peter Apian, *Introductio Geographica* (Ingolstadt, 1533), title page. Houghton (f*GC5.Ap34.533i2). **p. 30** Telescope attributed to Galileo. Courtesy of the Istituto e Museo di Storia della Scienza, Florence (2428). **p.31** Diagram illustrating eclipse of one of Jupiter's satellites, from James Ferguson, *Astronomy Explained* (London, 1756), plate 4, p.79. Houghton (*EC75.F3813.756a). **p.32** Table predicting the positions of Jupiter's satellites, from Giovanni Domenico Cassini, *Ephemerides Bononienses Mediceorum Syderum* (Bologna, 1668), p.2 of section entitled "Ephemerides Mediceorum Ad Annum MDCXVIII." Houghton (*IC6 C2735 668e). **p.33** Portrait of Giovanni Domenico (Jean-Dominique) Cassini (1625-1712) by Durangel, 1879, after an engraving based on a contemporary portrait. Courtesy of the Observatoire de Paris (inv. no. PPo5). **p.34** Louis XIV and Jean Baptiste Colbert, from C. Perrault, *Mémoires pour servir à l'histoire naturelle des animaux* (Amsterdam, 1736), frontispiece. Houghton (*FP6 Ac121 B736m v.1). **p.35** Delineations of French coastline, from Jean Picard and Philippe de La Hire, "Pour la Carte de France corrigée sur les Observations de MM. Picard & de La Hire," published in *Recueil d'Observations* (Paris, 1693), pp.91-92. Houghton (*f FC6 Ac121 693r). Computer-generated map by Jeffrey L. Ward Graphic Design. **p.36** Engraving of the Paris Observatory by Perelle, c. 1671. Courtesy of the Observatoire de Paris. **p.36** Contemporary portrait of Ole Roemer (1644-1710) at the Astronomical Observatory, University of Copenhagen. Ectachrome from the Ole Roemer Museum, Kroppedals Allé 3, DK-2630, Taastrup. **p.37** Diagram explaining Roemer's determination of the finite velocity of light, from James Ferguson, *Astronomy Explained* (London, 1756), plate 5, p.87. Houghton (*EC75.F3813.756a). **p.37** Ole Roemer in his observatory, from Peter Horrebow, *Basis Astronomiae sive Astronomiae pars Mechanica* (Havniae, 1735), plate III. Houghton (*QDC7 H7587 735B). **p.38** Portrait of King Charles II (1630-85) by Marcellus Laroon, c. 1670. Courtesy of Christ's Hospital (Blue Coat School). **p.39** Oil portrait of John Flamsteed (1646-1719), artist unknown, c. 1680, RS. **p.40** "Prospectus Versus Londinum" ("Prospect toward London"), an etching by Francis Place, c. 1676. From *London & Westminster, volume 1*, a book of topographical prints compiled by Samuel Pepys in 1700. Courtesy of the Pepys Library, Magdalene College, Cambridge. **p.41** "Prospectus Intra Camera Stellata" ("Prospect within the Star Chamber," now known as the Octagon Room), an etching by Francis Place, c. 1676. From *London & Westminster, volume 1*, a book of topographical prints compiled by Samuel Pepys in 1700. Courtesy of the Pepys Library, Magdalene College, Cambridge.

## Chapter Four
**p.42** Portrait of Gemma Frisius (1508-55) by Jan van Stalburch, 1557. Courtesy of the Ashmolean Museum, Oxford (Douce Collection: Solander 15, Mount 1). **p.44** Drum-shaped portable mechanical timekeeper, signed "Beauvais," France, c. 1540, TM (1070). **p.45** Drawing of Galileo's pendulum-controlled mechanism, 1659. Courtesy of the Biblioteca Nazionale Centrale (Manoscritti Galileiani, Galileo, p. VI, tome 4, c. 50). **p.46** Pastel portrait of Christiaan Huygens (1629-95) by Bernard Vaillant (1632-98). Courtesy of the Huygensmuseum Hofwijck, Voorburg, the Netherlands. **p.47** Sketch of pendulum drawn by Christiaan Huygens in his letter of March 28, 1658, to Jean Chapelain in Paris. Courtesy of the Department of Western Manuscripts, University Library, Leiden. **p.47** Pendulum clock by Salomon Coster, The Hague, 1657. TM (1131). **p.48** Drawing of a marine timekeeper, from Christiaan Huygens, *Horologium Oscillatorium* (Paris, 1673), p.20. Houghton (*fNC6 H9846 673h [B]). **p.49** Portrait of Robert Hooke (1635-1703) by Anders Hedberg, December 1997. Courtesy of Anders Hedberg. **p.49** Christiaan Huygens's first sketch of a balance spring, made in Paris on January 20, 1675. Courtesy of the Department of Western Manuscripts, University Library, Leiden.

## Chapter Five

**p.50** Portrait of William Whiston (1667-1752) by Sarah Hoadly, c. 1700(?). NPG (243). **p.52** Title page from Sir Kenelm Digby, *A Late Discourse Made in a Solemne Assembly of Nobles and Learned Men at Montpellier, France* (London, 1658). Houghton (*EC65.D5693.Eg658w). **p.53** Mezzotint of Sir Kenelm Digby (1603-65) by Jacob Houbraken, published in 1748, after a painting by Anthony van Dyke. Courtesy of the Collection of Historical Scientific Instruments, Harvard University (1998-1-0617). **p.54** Illustration of use of the cross-staff, from G. Willemsen van Hollesloot, *Die Caerte vande Oost ende Westzee* (1594). Courtesy of the Nederlands Scheepvaartmuseum, Harlingen, the Netherlands. **p.54** A Christ's Hospital boy using a backstaff, from Sir Jonas Moore, *A New Systeme of the Mathematicks* (London, 1681), pp.248-49. Houghton (*EC65.M7846.681n). **p.55** Azimuth compass by Edward Nairne, London. Courtesy of the Collection of Historical Scientific Instruments, Harvard University (95). **p.56** Edmond Halley's isogonic chart of the Atlantic, 1701. By permission of the William Andrews Clark Memorial Library, University of California, Los Angeles (MAP G9101 C93 1700 H34). Photograph courtesy of Rand McNally. **p.58** Title page from Samuel Fyler, *Longitudinis Inventae Explicatio* (London, 1699). Houghton (*EC65 F9936 699l). **p.60** Title page from William Whiston and Humphry Ditton, *A New Method for Discovering the Longitude* (London, 1714). Houghton (*EC7 W5794 714n). **p.60** Explanatory diagram for proposed longitude method, from William Whiston and Humphry Ditton, *A New Method for Discovering the Longitude* (London, 1714). Houghton (*EC7 W5794 714n).

## Chapter Six

**p.62** Portrait of Edmond Halley (c. 1656-1742) by Thomas Murray, not dated (but the illustration that Halley is holding may be identified with two important papers that he published in 1687). RS. **p.64** Portrait of Isaac Newton (1642-1727) attributed to John Vanderbank, c. 1726. NPG (558). **p.65** Title page from the Longitude Act of 1714 (Act 12 Anne *cap.* 15). By permission of the Harvard Law School Library, Harvard University (UK 353 E23). **p.65** Page from the Longitude Act of 1714 (Act 12 Anne *cap.* 15). By permission of the Harvard Law School Library, Harvard University (UK 353 E23). **p.68** Title page from Jane Squire, *A Proposal To Determine our Longitude*, 2d ed. (London, 1743). Houghton (*EC7 Sq584 742pb). **p.69** Illustration of proposed longitude method, from Jane Squire, *A Proposal To Determine our Longitude*, 2d ed. (London, 1743), folding plate opposite p.5. Houghton (*EC7 Sq584 742pb). **p.70** Title page from Jeremy Thacker, *The Longitudes Examin'd* (London, 1714). Courtesy of the British Library (533.f.22 [1]). **p.71** Engraving of Jeremy Thacker's chronometer, from his pamphlet, *The Longitudes Examin'd* (London, 1714). Courtesy of the British Library (533.f.22 [1]).

## Chapter Seven

**p.74** Wooden movement of Harrison's 1713 clock, in the collection of the Worshipful Company of Clockmakers, London. NMM (ref. D6769). **p.77** Map of England, from Ogilby, *Traveller's Guide* (London, 1730), printed for Thomas Bowles. Details of Wakefield and Barton areas, from Emanuel Bowen, *The Large English Atlas* (London, 1777), Map 41 (West Riding of Yorkshire, 1750) and Map 21 (Lincolnshire, 1751). Courtesy of the Harvard Map Collection, Harvard University (150.1730.2 and MA-LC G1808.B62.1777 PF*). **p.78** John Harrison's transcript of a lecture by Professor Saunderson, from Henry Sotheran and Co. catalogue, *Bibliotheca Chemico-Mathematica*, vol. 2 (London, 1921), No. 8960, facing p.454. Houghton (HRR 800 8). **p.79** Dial of Harrison's 1715 clock. Author's photograph. **p.79** Backplate of Harrison's 1715 clock. Author's photograph. **p.80** The equation of time table, by John Harrison, (1693-1776), pasted to the inside of his pendulum clock of 1717. WCC/Bridgeman. **p.82** View of stable clock built by John Harrison at Brocklesby Park c. 1722. By kind permission of the Earl of Yarborough. Photograph by Heather Lees,

courtesy of Lincolnshire County Council: Usher Gallery, Lincoln, UK. **p.83** Movement of stable clock at Brocklesby Park. By kind permission of the Earl of Yarborough. Photograph by Heather Lees, courtesy of Lincolnshire County Council: Usher Gallery, Lincoln, UK. **p.84** Illustration showing the area of an oak log used in the construction of the wheels of Harrison's clocks. Illustration by and courtesy of David Penney. **p.85** X-ray showing construction of one of the wooden wheels of Harrison's clocks. Courtesy of Andrew King. **p.86** Construction of Harrison's gridiron pendulum. Illustration by and courtesy of David Penney. **p.87** Precision longcase clock, c. 1725-26, made by John Harrison's brother James. TM (2000). **p.87** Side view of Harrison's precision longcase clock, c. 1725-26. TM (2000). **p.88** Action of Harrison's grasshopper escapement. Illustration by and courtesy of David Penney. **p.89** Backplate of Harrison's precision longcase clock, c. 1725-26. TM(2000). **p.90** Detail of Harrison's cottage in Barrow upon Humber, c. 1910. Photograph by George Schofield, courtesy of Andrew King. **p.90** Detail of Harrison's cottage in Barrow upon Humber, c. 1960. Photograph by George Schofield, courtesy of Andrew King. **p.91** The equation of time table, by John Harrison (1693-1776), on the frame of the door of his pendulum clock of 1728. WCC/Bridgeman.

## Chapter Eight

**p.92** Front view of H-1. NMM (D6783). **p. 94** First page of a document written by John Harrison concerning his ideas for making accurate clocks for use on land and sea, 1730. WCC/Bridgeman (MS6026/1). **p.94** Final page of a document written by John Harrison concerning his ideas for making accurate clocks for use on land and sea, 1730. WCC/Bridgeman (MS6026/1). **p.95** Mezzotint of George Graham (c. 1674-1751) by J. Faber, after the portrait by Thomas Hudson, TM (1198). **p.97** View of H-1 from above. NMM (D6783). **p.100** Detail of map showing the entrance to the English Channel, from Herman Moll, *The World described* (London, 1709-20), Map 3 (c. 1710). Houghton (*92J-100b PF). **p.102** Detail of inscription on H-2. Author's photograph. **p.103** Front view of H-2. NMM (D6784A). **p.104** Side view of movement of H-2. Author's photograph. **p.105** Drawing of H-3's balances from one of Harrison's manuscripts. Author's photograph. WCC/Bridgeman (MS3972/2, p. 13). **p.105** Detail of the longitude lunatic in "Bedlam," the last of eight prints of William Hogarth's *The Rake's Progress*, 1735. Courtesy of the Harvard University Art Museum; gift of Belinda L. Randall from the collection of John Witt Randall (R5694).

## Chapter Nine

**p.106** Portrait of John Hadley (1682-1744) by Bartholomew Dandridge (1691-c. 1755), c. 1730. NMM (BHC2731). **p.108** Sketch of mariner using an octant, from the log of Archibald Hamilton. NMM (B5327). **p.111** Octant dated 1750. Courtesy of the Collection of Historical Scientific Instruments, Harvard University (5303). **p.112** Portrait of James Bradley (1693-1762) by Thomas Hudson (1701-79). RS. **p.113** Lacaille's star map, 1752. Courtesy of the British Library (Maps141.a.1.[20]). **p.114** Portrait of Tobias Mayer (1723-62) by Westermayr. From Franz Xaver von Zach, *Allgemeine Geographische Ephemeriden Verfasset von einer Gesellschaft Gelehrten und herausgegeben*, vol. 3 (Weimar, 1799), frontispiece. Houghton (Harvard Depository KD 4484). **p.115** Portrait of Leonhard Euler (1707-83) by Emanuel Handmann, 1756. Photo: Öffentliche Kunstsammlung Basel, Martin Bühler. Courtesy of the Öffentliche Kunstsammlung Basel, Aulabilder. **p.116** Letter from Tobias Mayer to the Board of Longitude. Courtesy of Göttingen University Library (Hannover Des 92 XXXIV, No. II, 4, a1, p.62). **p.116** Title page from Tobias Mayer, *Tabulae Motuum Solis* (London, 1770). Houghton (*EC7 H1552 749aaa [D]). **p.117** Mariner taking a lunar distance measurement, from E. Dunkin, *The Midnight Sky* (London, 1869), p. 242. Houghton (Astr 8178.3). **p.118** Sextant with the Board of Longitude mark "D32" by Jesse Ramsden, c. 1772. Private collection.

## Chapter Ten

p.120 General view of H-3. NMM (D6785). p.122 Dies used to strike the Royal Society's Copley Medal. RS. p.123 Oil portrait of William Harrison (1728-1815) or his son John (1761-1842). Photograph courtesy of Lew and Pat Goodman. p.124 Instructions written by John Harrison for the assemby of his H-3 timekeeper. WCC/Bridgeman (MS3972/3, item 15). p.125 Illustration of H-3, probably drawn by Thomas Bradley, c. 1840. By permission of the Syndics of Cambridge University Library and the Director of the Royal Greenwich Observatory (MS. RGO 6/586 f213). p.126 Bi-metallic strip used in H-3. Illustration by and courtesy of David Penney. p.127 Watch by John Jefferys, (1752-53), London. WCC/Bridgeman (WCC71009). p.128 John Harrison's design for the "lesser watch," mentioned by him to the Board of Longitude on 19 June 1755, from a set of mechanical notes and drawings compiled by John and his son William, c. 1726-72. WCC/Bridgeman (WCC106103). p.129 Drawing of the layout of the movement of the timekeeper H-4 by John Harrison (1693-1776). WCC/Bridgeman (WCC106112). p.130 Design for a large enamel watch dial, from mechanical notes and drawings compiled by John Harrison (1693-1776) and his son William c. 1726-72. WCC/Bridgeman (WCC106102). p.131 General view of H-4. NMM (D789A). p.132 View of backplate of H-4. NMM (D789B). p.134 H-4 at the time of its exhibition at the U.S. Naval Observatory in Washington, D.C., in 1963-64. Photograph courtesy of Andrew King.

## Chapter Eleven

p.136 Portrait of Nevil Maskelyne (1732-1811) by Louis François Gérard Van de Puyl, 1785. RS. p.139 Diagram showing determination of sun's parallax by the transit of Venus, from James Ferguson, *Astronomy Explained* (London, 1764), plate 15, p. 319. Houghton (*EC75.F3813.756ac). p.141 Engraving of Portsmouth harbor, c. 1760. NMM (A3371). p.143 The first trial voyage of H-4. Illustration by Jeffrey L. Ward Graphic Design. p.144 Illustration of an astronomer's tent, engraved by J. Basire, published in W. Wales & W. Bayly, *The Original Astronomical Observations* (London, 1777), foldout plate opposite p. xii. Houghton (*f EC75.W1488.777o). p.145 Octant presented to William Harrison by Captain Dudley Digges in 1762. NMM (2097). p.146 Title page from Nevil Maskelyne, *The British Mariner's Guide* (London, 1763). Houghton (*EC75 M3795 763b). p.147 Portrait of Nathaniel Bliss (1700-64). NMM (BHC4144). p.148 The second trial voyage of H-4. Illustration by Jeffrey L. Ward Graphic Design.

## Chapter Twelve

p.150 Portrait of John Harrison (1693-1776) by Thomas King, c. 1766. Courtesy of the Science Museum, Science and Society Picture Library, London (1884-217). p.153 Mezzotint of John Harrison by Philippe Tassaert, 1768, after the portrait by Thomas King. TM (2494). p.155 First page of the Longitude Act of 1765 (Act 5 George III *cap.* 20). By permission of the Harvard Law School Library, Harvard University (UK 353 E23). p.157 Title page from the *Nautical Almanac* (London, 1769). Houghton (*85-77). p.158 Lunar distance table for August 1769 from the *Nautical Almanac* (London, 1768). Houghton (*85-77). p.159 Title page from *Tables Requisite*, 2d ed. (London, 1781). Houghton (NAV 637.81). pp.160-61 The Royal Observatory at Greenwich, c. 1766. NMM (C3807). p.162 Portrait of John Harrison (1693-1776) (enamel paste) by James Tassie (1735-99), c. 1775. WCC/Bridgeman (WCC106122).

## Chapter Thirteen

p.164 Portrait of Captain James Cook (1728-79) from an oil painting by Nathaniel Hodges (1744-97), who sailed with Cook on his second voyage. NMM (BHC4227). p.166 Detail from log book used by Captain Cook on his second voyage. By permission of the Syndics of Cambridge University Library and the Director of the Royal Greenwich Observatories (RGO 14/59, fol. 13). p.168 Pastel portrait of William Wales (1734-98) by John Russell, 1794. NMM (2625). p.170 General view of K-1. NMM (C9303A). p.170 View of backplate of K-1. NMM (C9303B). p.171 H-5 in its padded box.

WCC/Bridgeman (WCC71015). p.172 Backplate and case of H-5. WCC/Bridgeman (WCC71017). p.174 Portrait of King George III (1738-1820) by Johann Zoffany, c. 1771-72. Courtesy of the Royal Collection © Her Majesty the Queen. p.176 King George III's private observatory in Richmond Park, from George Ernest Papendiek, *Kew Gardens: A Series of Twenty-Four Drawings on Stone* (London, c. 1820). Courtesy of the Yale Center for British Art, Paul Mellon Collection (QK73/K4/P3). p.177 First page of the Longitude Act of 1774 (Act 14 George III *cap.* 66). By permission of the Harvard Law School Library, Harvard University (UK 353 E23).

## Chapter Fourteen

p.178 Thomas Mudge's first marine timekeeper. By permission of the Trustees of the British Museum (CAI-2119). p.180 Pierre Le Roy's "montre marine A." Courtesy of the Musée des Arts et Métiers, Paris/Photo Studio CNAM. p.180 Pastel portrait of Ferdinand Berthoud (1727-1807) by Louis René Vialy, 1752. Courtesy of the Musée des Arts et Métiers, Paris/Photo Studio CNAM. p.181 Frontispiece from Ferdinand Berthoud, *Traité des Horloges Marines* (Paris, 1773). Houghton (*f FC7 B4615 773t). p.182 General view of K-2. NMM (A5510). p.182 Backplate of K-2. NMM (A5511). p.183 Aquatint of the mutiny on the *Bounty* by Robert Dodd (1748-1816), c. 1790. NMM (B1337). p.184 Mezzotint of Thomas Mudge (1715-94) by C. Townley, 1772, after Nathaniel Dance. TM (368d). p.186 Mezzotint of John Arnold (1735-99) by Susan Esther Reid, after the portrait of c. 1787 by Robert Davy (1735?-93). TM (368c). p.188 Marine chronometer no. 32/122 made by John Arnold and Son in 1792. TM (795). p.189 Movement of Arnold chronometer no. 32/122, made in 1792. TM (795). p.190 Original patent drawing for Arnold's spring detent escapement, 1782 (no. 1328). Courtesy of the Patent Office, London. p.191 Original patent drawing for Earnshaw's spring detent escapement, 1783 (no. 1354). Courtesy of the Patent Office, London. p.192 Mezzotint of Thomas Earnshaw (1749-1829) by Samuel Bellin, after the portrait of 1798 by Martin Archer Shee (1769-1850). TM (368a). p.193 Earnshaw spring detent escapement watch signed "Wright in the Poultry, London, No. 2228," 1784. Private collection. p.193 Movement of Earnshaw spring detent escapement watch signed "Wright in the Poultry, London, No. 2228," 1784. Private collection. p.194 Marine chronometer no. 928 by Thomas Earnshaw, c. 1812. TM (350). p.195 Marine chronometer by Charles Frodsham, London, no. 1842, c. 1841. By kind permission of Charles Frodsham & Co. Ltd., London. p.195 Marine chronometer by A. Lange & Söhne, Glashütte B/Dresden, no. 203 975-B, made in 1944. TM (1728).

## Chapter Fifteen

p.196 The prime meridian of the world, c. 1997. NMM (D6854). p.198 Views of the Royal Greenwich Observatory, from *The Graphic*, August 8, 1885, pp.158-59. Courtesy of the Harvard College Library, Harvard University (HD p.2021). p.199 Time ball at the Royal Greenwich Observatory, c. 1870. NMM (D5607). p.200 Gate clock and time ball at the Royal Greenwich Observatory, c. 1950. NMM (A1681C). p.201 Detail of the U.S. Naval Observatory Alternate Master Clock at Falcon Air Force Base in Colorado. Courtesy of Fiftieth Space Wing Public Affairs, Falcon Air Force Base, Colorado. p.202 Photograph of Rupert Gould (1890-1948) with H-2. Courtesy of the National Association of Watch and Clock Collectors, Columbia, Pa (from NAWCC Bulletin, vol. 4, no. 4 [June 1950], p. 161). p.203 H-1 before restoration, c. 1920. By kind permission of Charles Frodsham & Co. Ltd., London. p.204 H-2 before restoration, c. 1920. By kind permission of Charles Frodsham & Co. Ltd., London. p.204 H-3 before restoration, c. 1920. By kind permission of Charles Frodsham & Co. Ltd., London. p.205 Page from Rupert Gould's notebook, c. 1935. NMM (MS GOU/4, Neg. 8456). p.207 Harrison's grave in St. John's, Hampstead. Author's photograph. p.208 Harrison gallery at the Old Royal Observatory. NMM (D7059).

# Bibliography

Andrewes, William J. H., ed. *The Quest for Longitude.* Cambridge, Massachusetts: Collection of Historical Scientific Instruments, Harvard University, 1996.

Andrewes, William J. H., and Atwood, Seth. *The Time Museum.* Rockford, Illinois: The Time Museum, 1984.

Angle, Paul M. *The American Reader.* New York: Rand McNally, 1958.

Asimov, Isaac. *Asimov's Biographical Encyclopedia of Science and Technology.* New York: Doubleday, 1972

Baillie, G. H. *Clocks and Watches: An Historical Bibliography.* Vol. 1. London: N. A. G. Press, 1951; rpt. London: Holland Press, 1978.

Barrow, Sir John. *The Life of George Lord Anson.* London: John Murray, 1839.

Bedini, Silvio A. *The Pulse of Time: Galileo Galilei, the Determination of Longitude, and the Pendulum Clock.* Firenze: Bibliotecca di Nuncius, 1991.

Betts, Jonathan. *Harrison.* London: National Maritime Museum, 1993.

_____. Introduction to *Principles and Explanations of Timekeepers by Harrison, Arnold and Earnshaw.* [Upton, Notts., England]: British Horological Institute, 1984.

Boorstin, Daniel J. *The Discoverers.* 2 vols. New York: Harry N. Abrams, 1983.

Brown, Lloyd A. *The Story of Maps.* Boston: Little, Brown, 1949.

Cardinal, Catherine, ed. *Ferdinand Berthoud, 1727-1807: Horloger mécanicien du Roi et de la Marine.* La Chaux-de-Fonds, Switzerland: Musée International d'Horlogerie, 1984.

Chapman, Allan. *Dividing the Circle: The Development of Critical Angular Measurement in Astronomy, 1500-1850.* 2d ed. Chicester, England: John Wiley & Sons in association with Praxis Publishing, 1995.

Clifton, Gloria. *Directory of British Scientific Instrument Makers, 1550-1851.* London: Zwemmer (with the National Maritime Museum), 1995.

Clutton, Cecil, and Daniels, George. *Clocks and Watches: The collection of the Worshipful Company of Clockmakers.* London: Sotheby Parke Bernet, 1975.

Daniels, George. *Watchmaking.* London: Sotheby Publications, 1981.

Dutton, Benjamin. *Navigation and Nautical Astronomy.* Annapolis: U.S. Naval Institute, 1951.

Earnshaw, Thomas. *Longitude: An Appeal to the Public.* London: 1808, rpt. British Horological Institute, 1986.

*English Maritime Books Printed Before 1801 Relating to Ships, Their Construction and Their Operation at Sea....* Compiled by Thomas R. Adams and David W. Waters. Providence, Rhode Island: The John Carter Brown Library, and Greenwich, England: The National Maritime Museum, 1995.

Espinasse, Margaret. *Robert Hooke.* London: Heinemann, 1956.

Gould, Rupert T. *John Harrison and His Timekeepers.* London: National Maritime Museum, 1978. (Reprinted from *The Mariner's Mirror*, Vol. XXI, No. 2, April 1935.)

_____. *The Marine Chronometer.* London: J. D. Potter, 1923; rpt. Antique Collectors' Club, 1989.

Heaps, Leo. *Log of the Centurion.* London: Hart-Davis, MacGibbon, 1973.

Hobden, Heather, and Hobden, Mervyn. *John Harrison and the Problem of Longitude.* Lincoln, England: Cosmic Elk, 1988.

Howse, Derek. *Greenwich Time and the Longitude.* New ed. London: Philip Wilson Publishers, 1997.

_____. *Nevil Maskelyne, The Seaman's Astronomer.* Cambridge, England: Cambridge University Press, 1989.

Howse, Derek, and Hutchinson, Beresford. *The Clocks and Watches of Captain James Cook, 1769-1969.* London: Antiquarian Horological Society, 1969.

[King, Andrew]. *From a Peal of Bells: John Harrison, 1693-1776.* Usher Gallery exhibition catalogue. [Lincoln, England]: Lincolnshire County Council, 1993.

Landes, David S. *Revolution in Time.* Cambridge, Mass.: Harvard University Press, 1983.

Laycock, William. *The Lost Science of John "Longitude" Harrison.* Kent, England: Brant Wright, 1976.

Le Bot, Jean. *Les chronomètres de marine français au XVIIIᵉ siècle, quand l'art de naviguer devenait science.* Grenoble, France, 1983.

Macey, Samuel L., ed. *Encyclopedia of Time.* New York: Garland, 1994.

May, W. E. *A History of Marine Navigation.* Henley-on-Thames, England: G. T. Foulis, 1973.

_____. "How the Chronometer went to Sea," in *Antiquarian Horology*, March 1976, pp. 638-63.

Mercer, Vaudrey. *John Arnold and Son, Chronometer Makers, 1762-1843.* London: Antiquarian Horological Society, 1972.

Miller, Russell. *The East Indiamen.* Alexandria, Virginia: Time-Life, 1980.

Morison, Samuel Eliot. *The Oxford History of the American People.* New York: Oxford University Press, 1965.

Mörzer Bruyns, Willem. *The Cross-staff, History and Development of a Navigational Instrument.* Zutphen, the Netherlands: Walburg Instituut, 1994.

Moskowitz, Saul. "The Method of Lunar Distances and Technological Advance," presented at the Institute of Navigation, New York, 1969.

Pack, S. W. C. *Admiral Lord Anson.* London: Cassel, 1960.

Quill, Humphrey. *John Harrison, Copley Medalist, and the £20,000 Longitude Prize.* Sussex: Antiquarian Horological Society, 1976.

_____. *John Harrison, the Man Who Found Longitude.* London: Baker, 1966.

Randall, Anthony G. *The Technology of John Harrison's Portable Timekeepers.* Sussex: Antiquarian Horological Society, 1989.

Randall, Anthony G. *The Time Museum Catalogue of Chronometers.* Rockford, Illinois: The Time Museum, 1992.

Randall, Anthony G., and Good, Richard. *Catalogue of Watches in the British Museum.* London: British Museum, 1990.

Sabrier, Jean-Claude. *La longitude en mer à l'heure de Louis Berthoud et Henri Motel.* Geneva: Editions Antiquorum, 1993.

Sadler, D. H. *Man is not Lost: A record of two hundred years of astronomical navigation with the Nautical Almanac, 1767-1967.* London: Her Majesty's Stationery Office, 1968.

Stewart, Larry. *The Rise of Public Science: Rhetoric, Technology, and Natural Philosophy in Newtonian Britain, 1660-1750.* Cambridge, England: Cambridge University Press, 1993.

Tait, Hugh. *Catalogue of Watches in the British Museum.* Vol. 1, *The Stackfreed.* London: British Museum Publications, 1987.

Taylor, E. G. R. *The Haven-Finding Art: A History of Navigation from Odysseus to Captain Cook.* New ed. London: Hollis & Carter for the Institute of Navigation, 1971.

_____. *The Mathematical Practitioners of Hanoverian England, 1714-1840.* Cambridge, England: Cambridge University Press, 1966.

_____. *The Mathematical Practitioners of Tudor and Stuart England* [1485-1714]. Cambridge, England: Cambridge University Press, 1954.

Thrower, Norman J. W. *Maps and Civilization: Cartography in Culture and Society.* Chicago: University of Chicago Press, 1996.

_____, ed. *The Three Voyages of Edmond Halley in the* Paramore, *1698-1701.* 2 vols. Hakluyt Society Publications, 2d series, no. 156-57. London: Hakluyt Society, 1981.

Turner, Anthony J. *Early Scientific Instruments: Europe, 1400-1800.* London: Sotheby's Publications, 1987.

Turner, Gerard L'E. *Nineteenth-Century Scientific Instruments.* London: Philip Wilson Publishers for Sotheby's Publications, 1983.

Vaughn, Denys, ed. *The Royal Society and the Fourth Dimension: The History of Timekeeping.* Sussex: Antiquarian Horological Society, 1993.

Waters, David W. *The Art of Navigation in England in Elizabethan and Early Stuart Times.* London: Hollis & Carter, 1958; and New Haven: Yale University Press, 1958.

Whittle, Eric S. *The Inventor of the Marine Chronometer: John Harrison of Foulby.* Wakefield, England: Wakefield Historical Publications, 1984.

Williams, J. E. D. *From Sails to Satellites: The Origin and Development of Navigational Science.* Oxford, England: Oxford University Press, 1992.

Wood, Peter H. "La Salle: Discovery of a Lost Explorer," in *American Historical Review*, Vol. 89 (1984), pp. 294-323.

# Index

*Note: Page references to illustrations are in italics.*